Information Technology
Skills and Knowledge

for GNVQ Intermediate Core Skill in IT

Gregg Harris and Michael Hogan

Gregg Harris and Michael Hogan currently lecture on a variety of information technology courses at Skelmersdale College. They have, between them, many years of experience of delivering IT skills training to a wide range of students, from school leavers to senior managers. They also have wide ranging experience of using IT in solving practical business problems.

DP Publications Ltd
Aldine Place
London W12 8AW
1993

Dedication

This book is dedicated to all staff and students at the Ashurst Business and Management Centre.

Acknowledgments

Without the help of numerous people this book would never have been produced. We would like to thank our families for their support and patience, Catherine Tilley of DP Publications for assistance above and beyond the call of duty, Skelmersdale College for allowing us to trial the material, and everyone who offered advice. We would also like to express our thanks to the following companies who kindly assisted us with illustrations: Amstrad, Apple Computers, Intel, Claris, Microsoft, IBM, Aldus and Lotus.

A CIP catalogue record for this book is available from the British Library

ISBN 1 85805 028 6
Copyright G Harris and M Hogan © 1993

All rights reserved
No part of this publication may be reproduced, stored in a retrieval system, or transmitted in any form or by any means, electronic, mechanical, photocopying, recording, or otherwise, without the prior permission of the copyright owner.

Typeset by Kai Typesetting, Nottingham

Printed by
Ashford Colour Press
Gosport, Hampshire

Preface

Aim

This book provides an activity-based course text to meet all the requirements of the GNVQ Intermediate Mandatory Core Skills Unit in Information Technology, making it suitable for students on any of the GNVQ Intermediate units (eg Business, Leisure and Tourism, etc). It is also ideal as a practical workbook for any introductory information technology courses, such as City and Guilds and RSA, GCSE Information Technology, the Business Information Technology module of BTEC National and for GCSE Computer Studies when used in conjunction with a text such as C S French's *Computer Studies* (DP Publications 1993).

The book is not machine or software specific, but assumes access to a microcomputer or networked terminal with word processing, spreadsheet, database and graphics/DTP software.

Need

All GNVQs demand that students acquire the skills, knowledge and understanding to use information technology as a tool for performing practical tasks in whatever vocational field they aim to enter. This book meets the need for new material that comprehensively covers the specification for the Core Skills Unit at this level and that allows students to acquire skills and knowledge through practical problems in realistic contexts. The specific relationship between the text and the Core Skills specification is clearly illustrated in the Coverage Chart on pages vii and viii.

The problem-solving, hands-on approach of the text makes it ideal for the many schools and colleges that centre their IT courses around a computer workshop sessions. Students can progress through the book at their own pace, with minimum lecturer/teacher support. The structure (see below) also means it is equally suited to students who have no knowledge or experience of IT, and those who may have met some topics before in their prior studies and therefore wish only to demonstrate competence in these particular topics.

Structure of the book

The book is organised so that the student can first identify the problem and the need for an IT solution in an everyday work context, before coming to the necessary skills and knowledge to implement the solution. The integration of knowledge and skills in the solution to these tasks means that students never have to digest much theory before being able to sit at their terminals and produce the necessary documents.

There are four main sections:

Section 1 – Scenarios and related tasks – Stars and Stripes Footwear

This section is the driving force of the book and introduces students to the typical IT-related problems and decisions faced by all organisations. It is divided into 30 units, each tackling a specific area of IT, and each with a combination of short scenarios, tasks related to that scenario and an optional extended task at the end of the unit. The students tackle the tasks via the 'Help lines' that direct them to either the necessary knowledge (in the Section 2 Information Bank) or skills (Section 3 Skills Bank) they require for solving the problem. Students who already have the necessary skills and/or knowledge to solve that problem because they have, say, been taught word processing already at school, can ignore the Help line and simply do the task using their prior knowledge. Tasks can be used to generate evidence of competence at this level.

Most tasks do not require answers; those that do, have answers in an appendix.

Preface

Section 2 – Information Bank

This section contains the supporting knowledge appropriate to this introductory level. It is divided into the usual key topics of the subject, but is not intended to be read as a conventional textbook from start to finish. Students only read specific short sections as they are directed to from tasks in Section 1. Once students have worked through all the tasks in Section 1 they will have been directed to the whole of this section.

Section 3 – Skills Bank

This section contains the necessary graded exercises to enable students to develop skills in word processing, spreadsheets, databases and graphics/DTP. Again, students are directed to these exercises one by one, as they need them, from the tasks in Section 1. The exercises allow students to practise a technique before using it to answer the Section 1 task. The book encourages students to build up their own notes to record their systems' methods and procedures, which they will find very useful when tackling assignments or computer-based work from other disciplines.

Once students have worked through all the tasks in Section 1 they will have been directed to the whole of this section.

Section 4 - Assignments

This section contains a series of assignments that can be used to provide additional evidence of competence at this level. Guidance to lecturers for assessment of assignments is given in the accompanying Lecturers' Supplement.

Lecturers'/Teachers' Supplement

The Supplement gives guidance to lecturers regarding the assignments in Section 4. It is available free of charge to all lecturers adopting the book as their course text book (apply to the publishers by completing the form accompanying inspection copies, or by writing on college-headed paper giving details of course and expected student numbers).

How to use the book

This book is ideally suited to be used in a workshop situation, in which all students have access to a computer terminal for at least part of the session. Students should be directed to read through the introduction to Section 1 and then to work through the Section 1 units (ideally in sequence). They should go to the Section 2 Information Bank and Section 3 Skills Bank as directed after each task. In the few cases where answers to the tasks are not self evident, they will be given in an appendix on page 157. It will only be if a student has difficulty that he or she should need lecturer help.

The book could also be used to support a course of lectures or classroom-based sessions provided students also had regular access to computer terminals. If the course tackled the topics in a different order to the sequence of Section 1 units (see Contents page v), students could be directed to follow the units in this order as long as they were worked through in logical groups (ie all spreadsheets units tackled in sequence before tackling, say, word processing).

Lecturers can direct the quicker students to the extended tasks at the end of most units in Section 1, and the assignments in Section 4 can be set to assess competence.

September 1993

Contents

Preface	iii
GNVQ Syllabus Coverage	vii
Section 1 – Stars and Stripes Footwear – Scenarios and related tasks	1
Introduction to Stars and Stripes Footwear	4
1 Richard and Sarah discover IT	5
2 Investigating word processing	6
3 Storing information on a word processor	9
4 Producing a business letter	10
5 Producing a price list	12
6 Choosing a word processor	14
7 Richard uses his memory	15
8 Looking after the finances	16
9 Discovering spreadsheets	18
10 Using a spreadsheet	19
11 Producing invoices on a spreadsheet	20
12 Keeping financial records on a spreadsheet	22
13 Displaying information	23
14 Controlling the system	26
15 Keeping track of stock	27
16 Computerising the stock records	29
17 Amending the database	30
18 Interrogating the database	31
19 Using a database appropriately and effectively	32
20 Hard disks and other data storage media	33
21 Staying secure	34
22 Producing letterheads and logos	35
23 Page layout	36
24 Running complex programs	37
25 Saving time	38
26 Going into print	39
27 Keeping in touch	40
28 On-line	41
29 Extending expertise	42
30 Information technology applications	43
Section 2 – Information Bank	45
1 Information technology	46
2 Word processing	49
3 Floppy disk backing storage	54
4 Computer hardware	56
5 Spreadsheets	64

Contents

	6	Systems software	69
	7	Application software	71
	8	Databases	74
	9	Hard disks and other backing storage media	78
	10	Data security and safety	80
	11	Computer graphics	84
	12	Desk top publishing	87
	13	Input devices	90
	14	Output devices – printers	92
	15	Communication technology	94
	16	Accounting/Bookkeeping packages	99
	17	Integrated software	99
	18	Musical Instrument Digital Interface	101
	19	Further information technology applications	102

Section 3 – Skills bank — 105

Word processing exercises	106
Word processing systems notes	115
Spreadsheet exercises	118
Spreadsheet systems notes	125
Database exercises	129
Database systems notes	135
Graphics exercises	138
Graphics systems notes	144

Section 4 – Assignments — 147

1	Buying a computer	148
2	Communications	149
3	Evaluating equipment	150
4	IT in the business environment	151
5	Word processing	152
6	Spreadsheet	154
7	Database	155

Appendix Answers to tasks in Section 1 — 157

Index — 160

Coverage chart of GNVQ Intermediate IT Core Skills

The chart below is intended to help teachers/lecturers plan their courses and gauge students's progress towards completion of all GNVQ requirements.

It is not always possible to 'break down' performance criteria into just a few units, since they may be skills that can be demonstrated whenever technology is used by the student (these are indicated by ❖ in the chart below). Where units are shown it is for guidance only, since some criteria, *visual display* for instance, would require observation. It is also important to remember that the chart below is based on the student completing all tasks within a unit. It may also be the case, particularly in the assignments (Section 4), that students meet criteria that have not been specified. Certain criteria, such as 'organisation of storage systems allows applications to run efficiently...' can be addressed within the text, but are so system specific that they cannot be assessed within a textbook. It is suggested that the *Your own notes* sections of the *System notes* in Section 3 are used to list operating and fault reporting procedures. If this is done, then a record can also be kept of any faults and the action taken. This could supply evidence for Element 2.5. It must be stressed that the chart below is for guidance only, and it is for individual lecturers to satisfy themselves concerning adequacy and range.

	Sec. 1 Units	Sec. 2 Units	Sec. 3 Units	Sec. 4 Projects
Element 2.1: Set up storage systems and input information **Performance criteria:**				
1 information is entered in full and conforms to requirements/ conventions regarding labelling, format and place [within file(s)/record(s)]	❖	❖	❖	❖
2 information is entered using a format which will enable any subsequent editing to be carried out efficiently	❖		❖	❖
3 copies of drafts/source information are retained as directed	❖		❖	
4 the organisation of storage system allows efficient location, retrieval and transfer of information	❖			
5 security routines are used to protect information from accidental deletion/disruption and tampering		9 and 10		
Element 2.2: Edit, organise and integrate information **Performance criteria:**				
1 correct information is retrieved using retrieval routines	❖	❖	❖	❖
2 information is protected from accidental deletion/disruption and tampering	3, 20, 21	3, 9, 10		
3 unwanted information is removed and backup routines are implemented correctly		10		
4 editing/search/calculation routines minimise the number of steps/stages needed	❖	2, 5, 8	❖	5, 6, 7
5 editing/moving/copying routines minimise the risks of deleting/disrupting information	❖		❖	
6 information is saved/arranged in a form which makes it most amenable to transfer	27, 28, 29, 30	15, 17, 18, 19		
7 any discrepancies between the source material and new files/records are corrected if necessary	❖		❖	

Continued overleaf

	Sec. 1 Units	Sec. 2 Units	Sec. 3 Units	Sec. 4 Projects
Element 2.3: Select and use formats for presenting information **Performance criteria:**				
1 final version of information is legible, accurate and complete	❖		❖	❖
2 output/final presentation corresponds with requirements	❖		❖	❖
3 waste is minimised during production of hard copy	❖	14	❖	
4 format options are used to create a format which displays information effectively	❖	2, 5, 8, 11, 12	❖	❖
Element 2.4: Evaluate features and facilities of given applications **Performance criteria:**				
1 the importance of accuracy and precision when using information (IT) is explained	21	10		
2 the importance of using procedures which protect information from accidental deletion, disruption and tampering is explained	3, 20, 21	3, 9, 10		
3 the ways that features of given applications affect the efficiency of day working are described and evaluated	2, 4, 5, 6, 9, 13, 19, 23	2, 5, 7, 8, 11, 12, 16, 17, 18, 19,		
4 facilities offered by applications which can improve day-to-day working are evaluated, selected and used	2, 4, 5, 9–13, 15–18, 22, 23		❖	5, 6, 7
Element 2.5: Deal with errors and faults at intermediate level **Performance criteria:**				
1 information technology equipment is used in accordance with health and safety requirements	❖	9, 10	❖	❖
2 errors and faults are correctly identified and prompt action is taken	❖		❖	❖
3 errors and faults which fall outside own scope are referred to appropriate personnel promptly	❖		❖	❖
4 approaches used to rectify faults and errors do not cause harm to persons nor damage to equipment and stored information	❖		❖	❖
5 prompt action is taken to alert others to knock-on effect of identified errors and faults on their activities	❖		❖	❖

Section 1 Scenarios and related tasks

This section comprises 30 units that follow the way a small company, Stars and Stripes Footwear, discovers IT solutions to some of its day-to-day administrative problems. In this way, you will be able to meet the main applications of IT in the context in which you are most likely to meet them yourself when you start working.

The structure of each unit follows a common pattern:

- **Objectives of that unit** – ie what you will be able to do once you have completed the unit
- **Scenario** – always centred on Stars and Stripes Footwear
- **Tasks** – these enable you to find out about the IT application in question (by following up the cross reference to the appropriate part of the Section 2 Information Bank). If the task is a practical one, the cross reference to the Section 3 Skills Bank will enable you to carry out the task itself.

Many units also have an **extension task** which allows you to practise a skill further, or may require you to research a particular topic.

You are recommended to work through the units in the order they are presented, but you can tackle them by **topic**, eg work through (in sequence) all the units concerned with databases, before moving on to those concerned with, say, spreadsheets.

Before you start Unit 1 of this section, read carefully the *Introduction to Stars and Stripes Footwear* on page 4.

Section 1

Contents

Unit 1   Richard and Sarah discover IT   5
This unit introduces IT to the business environment and looks at how a variety of business activities process information, with a view to improving the efficiency of these activities.

Unit 2   Investigating word processing   6
This unit introduces the idea of improving the presentation of documents using word processors.

Unit 3   Storing information on the word processor   9
This unit introduces the idea of using floppy disks as a media for storing data.

Unit 4   Producing a business letter   10
In this unit you will use your skills to produce a business letter.

Unit 5   Producing a price list   12
In this unit you will produce a price list using your word processor.

Unit 6   Choosing a word processor   14
In this unit you find out what features to look for when purchasing a word processor.

Unit 7   Richard uses his memory   15
This unit introduces you to computer memory – RAM and ROM.

Unit 8   Looking after the finances   16
This unit looks at how financial calculations are performed manually.

Unit 9   Discovering spreadsheets   18
This unit introduces the idea of using spreadsheets to record and process financial information.

Unit 10   Using a spreadsheet   19
In this unit you will use a spreadsheet to create a spreadsheet document.

Unit 11   Producing invoices on a spreadsheet   20
In this unit you will use a spreadsheet to prepare a company invoice.

Unit 12   Keeping financial records on a spreadsheet   22
In this unit you will use a spreadsheet to help monitor the flow of money into and out of the business.

Unit 13   Displaying information   23
In this unit you will use the spreadsheet to display the information graphically.

Unit 14   Controlling the system   26
In this unit the operating system and the role it plays in the working of the computer is explained.

Unit 15   Keeping track of stock   27
In this unit you will create manual records of stock.

Stars and Stripes Footwear

Unit 16 Computerising the stock records   29
Introduces electronic computer databases for keeping stock records.

Unit 17 Amending the database   30
In this unit you will edit and make changes to the database stock file.

Unit 18 Interrogating the database   31
In this unit you will interrogate the electronic database file for stock information.

Unit 19 Using a database appropriately and effectively   32
In this unit the benefits of databases, together with their legal restrictions, are explained.

Unit 20 Hard disks and other data storage media   33
This unit introduces backing storage systems for data kept on computer.

Unit 21 Staying secure   34
This unit looks at the possible risks to data stored on computer, and what methods may be employed to prevent data loss. It also highlights health and safety considerations.

Unit 22 Producing letterheads and logos   35
In this unit you will use a graphics package to create a company logo.

Unit 23 Page layout   36
This unit introduces you to desktop publishing.

Unit 24 Running complex programs   37
This unit looks at different microprocessors and their applications.

Unit 25 Saving time   38
Bar codes are just among the few input devices dealt with in this unit.

Unit 26 Going into print   39
In this unit you are introduced to the different types of printing devices.

Unit 27 Keeping in touch   40
This unit introduces you to different types of communication technology.

Unit 28 On-line   41
In this unit you are shown how on-line information services may be of use to a small business.

Unit 29 Extending expertise   42
In this unit you are will learn about accounts packages, integrated software and MIDI systems.

Unit 30 Information technology applications   43
In this unit you will apply your knowledge of information technology to Richard's and Sarah's business and also look at how information technology affects society.

Section 1

Introduction to Stars and Stripes Footwear

Sarah Nugent and Richard Gordon started a small business six months ago with the help of money from a Government small business development grant. Through a friend, who works in America, they have started to import fashionable branded sports shoes and to sell them from their rented premises in Liverpool.

Like many small businesses, Stars and Stripes Footwear has been started with very little investment in equipment or skilled manpower, and Sarah and Richard are doing virtually everything in the business themselves. They have both been working very long hours and are convinced that they could be more efficient in the way that they handle and process customer orders and stock movements. In an effort to improve the way they organise themselves they decide to draw up a list of exactly what they do when they **process a customers order**:

1. **Receive customer orders**	Receive order. If it is a telephone order note down the details. Create a customer file with details of the goods ordered.
2. **Invoices**	Prepare and calculate customer invoices from customer orders. Keep records of outstanding debts with customer records.
3. **Stock Records**	Change levels of stock as customer orders are prepared and despatched. Stock files for each stock item are altered as items are reordered or despatched
4. **Remittances**	Record details of all payments received from customers in accounting books. Update customer file as payment is received.

They also draw up a list of their main business **objectives** in order to plan for the next six months of the business.

- ☐ Cut down on paperwork, especially that associated with order processing
- ☐ Expand their business by advertising and leafleting more extensively
- ☐ Increase the amount of mail order business the company does
- ☐ Improve the image of the company by producing professional looking documents for customer and supplier consumption
- ☐ Improve communications with customers and suppliers

Unit 1 Richard and Sarah discover IT

By the end of this unit you should have a better understanding of why businesses need information technology.

Scenario

One of the most important objectives in Richard's and Sarah's list of objectives (see *Introduction to Stars and Stripes Footwear* page 4) is to cut down on the very time-consuming paperwork that they do each day, as this will give them the time to achieve their other objectives (such as expanding their business).

Task 1 Look at their daily order processing routine (see *Introduction to Stars and Stripes Footwear* page 4), and categorise these jobs into those that mainly concern numbers (known as *numeric*) and those that are mainly text (called *alphabetic*), or those that contain a combination of both numbers and text (called *alphanumeric*).

Help? See Unit 1.1 Information Bank page 46.
Answer in Appendix page 157.

Task 2 Before Richard and Sarah can consider how to tackle these jobs more efficiently, they need to break each one down into the different operations involved.

Taking, one by one, each job you looked at in Task 1, complete the table below (the first one has been done for you) with each of the operations you think would be involved in doing that job successfully.

Help? See Unit 1.2 Information Bank page 46.
Answer in Appendix page 158.

Job	*Capture*	*Process*	*Store and retrieve*	*Communicate*
Receive order	Complete order form	Check items in stock and create customer file	Keep a copy of order for records and file in logical place	No communication unless query on order. List orders taken to pass on for despatch

Section 1

Unit 2 Investigating word processing

By the end of this unit you will know the advantages of using a word processor rather than a typewriter. You will be able to create a straightforward word processed document and save it on your computer.

Scenario

Sarah has been in touch with one of her old school friends, Rebecca Moore, who is now editor of a student magazine called *Ragtime News*. This magazine is published termly on a very low budget and sold in colleges throughout England and Wales.

Rebecca and Sarah have agreed an arrangement by which Rebecca will send out a leaflet about the business with each copy of the magazine in return for a small contribution towards the production costs of the magazine. It is a good opportunity for Stars and Stripes Footwear to reach new customers who would appreciate their low prices and up-to-date range.

Sarah begins producing it on the business's manual typewriter, and produces a letter to the readers of the magazine that looks like this:

```
                    Stars and Stripes Footwear
                          42 Dock Road
                            Liverpool
                             L4 8TG

September 1993

Dear Ragtime News reader

Are you fed up with turning up to parties in
trainers everyone else is wearing? Are you too
broke to pay for the trendiest trainers from high
street shops? If so, then we could be the answer.

Stars and Stripes Footwear offers the latest
American trainers at low prices because we buy from
USA and sell direct to you, without going through
shops. We get the latest lines before anyone else
in the country.

As a special offer to Ragtime News readers, we are
offering a 20% discount to all students who place
an order with us before January 1994, and to the
first 100 customers we are offering free laces in
any colour you want.

For a free catalogue and price list, with all
ordering information, phone us on 051 723 4689 or
write to Stars and Stripes Footwear, 42 Dock Road,
Liverpool, L4 8TG
```

Unit 2: Investigating word processing

Neither she nor Richard are happy that this will attract new customers or give an impression of a successful, professional business. Sarah shows the letter to Rebecca, who agrees that it is not very impressive, and she offers to redo it on her word processor. She comes up with the following version.

> **Stars and Stripes Footwear**
> 42 Dock Road
> Liverpool
> L4 8TG
>
> September 1993
>
> Dear **Ragtime News** reader
>
> Are you fed up with turning up to parties in trainers everyone else is wearing? Are you too broke to pay for the trendiest trainers from high street shops? If so, then we could be the answer.
>
> *Stars and Stripes Footwear* offers the **latest** American trainers at **low prices** because we buy from USA and sell direct to you, without going through shops. We get the latest lines before anyone else in the country.
>
> As a special offer to **Ragtime News** readers, we are offering a **20% discount** to all students who place an order with us before January 1994, and to the first 100 customers we are offering **free laces** in any colour you want.
>
> For a free catalogue and price list, with all ordering information, phone us on
>
> *051 723 4689*
>
> or write to
>
> *Stars and Stripes Footwear, 42 Dock Road, Liverpool, L4 8TG*

Task 1 Do you think that Rebecca has improved the presentation of the letter? List the specific improvements to layout and presentation that you can identify.

Help? See Unit 2.1 – 2.3 Information Bank page 49.

Section 1

Task 2   Using the breakdown of their daily routine given in the *Introduction to Stars and Stripes Footwear* (page 4), list those activities you think a word processor could help Richard and Sarah with.

Help? See Unit 1.1 Information Bank page 46.

Task 3   Word process the list produced in Task 1.

Help? See Unit 1 The Skills Bank page 106 to help you learn how to use your word processor. Read the introduction to the Skills Bank (page 105) first, and remember to build up your system notes (page 115) as you are doing the exercises.

Extension Task

Using your place of study or work as an example, compare how much material is produced by typewriter and how much is word processed, and look at the presentation of both outputs.

Unit 3 Storing information on a word processor

By the end of this unit, you will know how to organise and store information on a floppy disk.

Scenario

Impressed by the improvement in presentation achieved by the computer and printer, Sarah asks Rebecca how she and Richard could obtain this kind of equipment. Rebecca tells her that *Ragtime News* has an older computer that is not being used at the moment, and suggests that Sarah borrows it. When Richard and Sarah receive this computer on loan, it has with it a number of 3.5" disks (or floppy disks) holding word-processing, database and spreadsheet programs.

Task 1   How would you explain to Sarah and Richard what a floppy disk is?

          Help? See Unit 3.1 Information Bank page 54.

Task 2   What is meant by formatting or initialisation?

          Help? See Unit 3.2 Information Bank page 55.

Task 3   Why is the file address track very important?

          Help? See Unit 3.3 Information Bank page 55.

Task 4   How much data can they store on each floppy disk?

          Help? See Unit 3.4 Information Bank page 56.

Section 1

Unit 4 Producing a business letter

By the end of this unit you will know how to use a word processor to produce and edit a simple business letter.

Scenario

One morning, Sarah takes delivery of a consignment of footwear which is faulty. Unfortunately, she is preoccupied with other matters at the time and does not check the stock thoroughly, which she usually does. Only later does she discover that the stitching in some of the trainers is coming away and the upper parts of the trainers are torn. Sarah counts 24 pairs of faulty trainers altogether. She immediately repacks the faulty goods and drafts a letter to accompany the goods back to the supplier.

Stars and Stripes Footwear
42 Dock Road
Liverpool
L4 8TG

Mr T Goldstein
Atlantic Footwear
New York City
New York State
USA

September 1993

Dear Mr Goldstein

Re delivery note XCD4557M

I have just taken delivery of a consignment of goods, delivery note number XCD4557M. Unfortunately on delivery I was unable to check the stock thoroughly, and it was only later in the day that I discovered that 24 pairs of the consignment were faulty. As you can see the stitching has not been fully applied, and subsequently there is slight damage to the upper part of the shoes.

As you are no doubt aware, the number and type of trainers we buy from you are directly linked to the customer orders, therefore I would be very grateful if you could treat this matter with the greatest urgency so that our customers are not disappointed.

I have repackaged the goods and returned them to you in order that replacement stock can be issued.

Yours sincerely

Sarah Nugent

Sarah Nugent
Stars and Stripes Footwear Ltd

Enc. 24 pairs shoes and copy of delivery note number XCD4557M

Unit 4: Producing a business letter

Task 1 Key in the letter Sarah wants to send, check it is correct against her draft, and save the document as LETTER. On checking it, Sarah realises that it would be better if the last two paragraphs of the letter were transposed. Use the cut and paste facility on your word processor to amend the letter.

    Help? See Units 2 – 5 The Skills Bank page 107.
    Remember to build up your system notes (page 115) as you are doing the exercises

and see Unit 2.4 Information Bank page 50.

Task 2 When Sarah checks her letter against the delivery note, she realises she has transposed a couple of the digits, and that the correct number is XDC4575M. Use the edit facility on your word processor to change the numbers to the correct ones. Also, use the bold type facility to emphasise the subject of the letter.

    Help? See Units 2 – 5 The Skills Bank page 107.
    Remember to build up your system notes (page 115) as you are doing the exercises

and see Unit 2.2 Information Bank page 49.

Task 3 Save the letter and print out a copy, making sure that the text is positioned correctly on a sheet of A4 paper.

Use your system notes to help you do this

Extension task

Collect together a number of non-confidential business letters that arrive at your home each week. These may include advertisements from mail order catalogues, letters from banks advertising credit card facilities, etc. Look at the display format of the letters – are they all displayed in the same way? If they are different, how are they different, and which do you think are the more effective?

Section 1

Unit 5 Producing a price list

By the end of this unit, you will be able to use appropriate tabulation settings to produce a price list and make amendments to it.

Scenario

Sarah and Richard have had a call from a regular customer asking if they could send him a price list as he is often asked by friends where he buys his sports shoes, and what else is available. Sarah realises that it would be a good idea to send out a price list with every order to encourage customers to order something further, or pass the information on to a friend. When she tries to produce one on her typewriter, however, Sarah finds it very difficult to line up the columns of figures correctly.

Task 1 Which features of a word processor would help Sarah produce a clear price list?

Help? See Unit 2.5 Information Bank page 50.

Task 2 Using your word processor and the correct tabulation settings, enter the following price list, ensuring that you carefully proof read, correct, save and print your document

Help? See Units 6 – 8 The Skills Bank page 111.
Remember to build up your system notes page 115 as you are doing the exercises.

Stars and Stripes Footwear Ltd
Price list
This price list is valid, apart from taxation changes, until November 1993

Make	Model	Colour	Price
US Sports	Sonic	White/Purple	£29.99
US Sports	APS 2000	White/Blue	£55.99
US Sports	APS 3000	Red/Blue	£49.99
Apipco	Gazelle	Blue	£35.99
Apipco	Hurricane	Blue/Magenta	£45.99
Apipco	High Flier	Blue/Green	£29.99
PBS	High Shot	Blue/White	£49.99
PBS	Tornado	White	£55.99
SPX	Super 9	Blue/White	£49.99
SPX	Slapshot	White/Purple	£42.99
Streetlife	Dynamo 33	Purple	£19.99

Unit 5: Producing a price list

Task 3   Make the following amendments to the document
   a) Change the date of the price list to *until February 1994*
   b) Increase the price of the PBS Tornado to £69.99 and Apipco Hurricane to £49.99
   c) US Sports has changed its name to Americano. Use your search and replace facility to change all occurrences of the name in the price list.

Ensure that you save and print the document.

The price list should now look like this:

Stars and Stripes Footwear Ltd
Price list

This price list is valid, apart from taxation changes, until February 1994

Make	Model	Colour	Price
Americano	Sonic	White/Purple	£29.99
Americano	APS 2000	White/Blue	£55.99
Americano	APS 3000	Red/Blue	£49.99
Apipco	Gazelle	Blue	£35.99
Apipco	Hurricane	Blue/Magenta	£49.99
Apipco	High Flier	Blue/Green	£29.99
PBS	High Shot	Blue/White	£49.99
PBS	Tornado	White	£69.99
SPX	Super 9	Blue/White	£49.99
SPX	Slapshot	White/Purple	£42.99
Streetlife	Dynamo 33	Purple	£19.99

Help? See Unit 7 Skills Bank page 112 and Unit 2.2 Information Bank page 49.

Extension task

Collect and compare at least eight different sorts of tables that you come across, and for each one answer the following questions:

Is it easy to read? Why?

Is it easy to understand? Why?

Does it tell me what I might need to know? Should it have other information?

Could it be better laid out? How?

Section 1

Unit 6 Choosing a word processor

By the end of this unit you will know about some of the further features of, as well as the different types of, word processor. You will also know how to approach choosing the most suitable program for your needs.

Scenario

Both Richard and Sarah are so impressed by what the word processor can do that they consider buying their own, more up-to-date word processor, instead of using their borrowed machine.

Task 1   What further features should they look for when considering what word processor they require (try and evaluate which features would be useful to Stars and Stripes and which wouldn't be needed)?

Help? See Unit 2.6 Information Bank page 51.

Task 2   Prepare a short guide for them listing the main types of word processor and the features that they should look for (bearing in mind the requirements of the company).

Help? See Unit 2.7 Information Bank page 52.

Task 3   A friend suggests that they might want to run other applications on their computer. What does the friend mean by 'applications'?

Help? See Unit 7.1 Information Bank page 71.

Task 4   When choosing applications software what issues should be kept in mind?

Help? See Unit 7.2, 7.3 and 7.4 Information Bank page 72.

Extension task

Using your place of work/study as your subject, assess how well the word processor you are using meets your needs, particularly in the areas of

a) ease of use and learning

b) range of facilities – highlighting which are most useful to you

c) possible improvements or extra features you would like to see

Unit 7 Richard uses his memory

By the end of this unit you will understand what computer memory is, what types there are and why it is important.

Scenario

Richard and Sarah have been considering which word processor to buy. They decide to buy a computer that can run other applications in addition to wordprocessing, and visit a shop to see what is available. They don't want to spend too much money, and begin by looking at one of the cheapest on the market. The shop assistant helping them mentions that they should consider what uses they will put it to before choosing the hardware 'because it only has a RAM of 1 Mb' which he feels may be a problem.

Task 1   Explain for Richard what RAM is and how it is measured.

Help? See Unit 4.1 and 4.2 Information Bank page 56.

Task 2   What is the difference between RAM and ROM?

Help? See Unit 4.1 and 4.2 Information Bank page 56.

Task 3   Explain the major developments in computers that have made it possible for Richard and Sarah to consider buying their own computer.

Help? See Unit 4.3 Information Bank page 58.

Extension Task

Conduct a survey of your college/workplace, and find out the range of memory sizes that exist in the different types of computer around you. Is there a clear relationship between the size of the memory and the tasks performed by the different machines?

Section 1

Unit 8 Looking after the finances

By the end of this unit, you will be familiar with using a calculator for simple business calculations.

Scenario

Sarah and Richard are finding that, as their business grows, they are having to spend more and more time calculating such things as prices, stock levels, etc. They normally use a calculator as it is faster and more accurate than working out amounts in their heads.

Some calculations, however, take a considerable amount of time, even when made on a calculator. As they import most of their sports shoes they have to take account of various costs, including Value Added Tax (VAT), postage and packing and insurance. They also have to produce invoices for each customer order, keep a check on stock levels and on the amount of money going in and out of the business. Not surprisingly, they have found that the more calculations they have to do, the more likely they are to make mistakes, which can cost them money to correct.

Task 1 Using a calculator, work out and record the total cost of the following sports shoes:

Astro   £49.99
Tortillo   £39.99
Predator 5   £39.99
Gazelle   £35.99

Total

Answer in Appendix page 158.

Task 2 VAT is a percentage of the price of each pair of shoes. Assume that VAT is 17.5% and calculate the total amount of VAT that will have to be paid on the shoes in Task 1. (*Tip:* To find 17.5% of a number, multiply the number by .175)

Using a calculator, work out and record the VAT to be paid, and the total price, including VAT, of each of the following shoes:

Model	*Price*	*VAT*	*Total*
Slapshot	£42.99	?	?
Super 9	£49.99	?	?
Trident	£39.99	?	?
Terminator	£49.99	?	?

Answer in Appendix page 158.

Unit 8: Looking after the finances

Task 3   The insurance is always 2% of the price that Sarah and Richard sell the shoes for, so it is based on the price *including* VAT. (*Tip* To find 2% of a number, multiply the number by .02)

Using a calculator, work out and record the total cost including VAT and insurance, of the following shoes:

Model	Price	VAT	Insurance	Total
Slapshot	£42.99	?	?	?
Super 9	£49.99	?	?	?
Trident	£39.99	?	?	?
Terminator	£49.99	?	?	?

(Remember that your answer to *Task 2* already includes VAT)

Answer in Appendix page 158.

Section 1

Unit 9 Discovering spreadsheets

By the end of this unit, you will know the advantages of using a computer to perform financial calculations and basic principles of how a spreadsheet program works.

Scenario

Sarah and Richard feel that using a calculator is a very time-consuming way of working out their finances. They realise that they are often doing very repetitive calculations, such as working out VAT and insurance, where the only variable numbers are the prices of the shoes (the VAT rate and the insurance percentage are constant at 17.5% and 2% respectively).

They feel that their computer should be able to help, and their friend Rebecca tells them that there is a type of program, called a *spreadsheet*, which they will find very useful.

Task 1 In what way do you think a spreadsheet may be of use to Richard and Sarah?

Help? See Unit 5.1 Information Bank page 64.

Task 2 Explain the different types of data that can be entered into a spreadsheet and what is meant by the term 'formatting'.

Help? See Unit 5.2 Information Bank page 65.

Task 3 Explain the importance of spreadsheet formulae. Why is it crucial to enter formulae accurately when creating a spreadsheet?

Help? See Unit 5.3 Information Bank page 65.

In an effort to increase their profits, Sarah considers raising the prices of certain styles of shoes, but at the same time offering a discount to customers buying two or more pairs of any of the styles. She needs to know exactly how these two changes would affect the company's profits for a typical month before deciding whether or not to go ahead.

Task 4 What features of a spreadsheet could help her reach a decision, and what else could she use them for?

Help? See Unit 5.4 Information Bank page 66.

Task 5 Using your computer, create a spreadsheet to add up the following shoe prices:

Astro	£49.99
Tortillo	£39.99
Predator 5	£39.99
Gazelle	£35.99
Total	

Help? See Units 9–10 Skills Bank page 118.

Extension task

Using your spreadsheet as an example, find out how many automatic functions (types of calculation) your spreadsheet has built into its memory.

Unit 10 Using a spreadsheet

By the end of this unit you will be able to construct a computer spreadsheet using formulae. You will also know which features you should consider when choosing a spreadsheet program.

Scenario

Sarah and Richard decide to put their price lists on a spreadsheet.

Task 1   Using your computer, construct a spreadsheet that will calculate the costs of the following order. Remember to calculate the costs for each pair of shoes and also the totals for *VAT, insurance, total price* and the overall total of the order. The order is as follows:

Model	Price	VAT	Insurance	Quantity	Total
Slapshot	£42.99	?	?	1	?
Super 9	£49.99	?	?	1	?
Trident	£39.99	?	?	1	?
Terminator	£49.99	?	?	1	?
Astro	£49.99	?	?	1	?
Tortillo	£49.99	?	?	1	?
Predator 5	£39.99	?	?	1	?
Gazelle	£35.99	?	?	1	?
Total		?	?		?

Help? See Unit 10–12 Skills Bank page 119.

Task 2   How large could Richard make this spreadsheet (use your own as an example)?

Task 3   Sarah decides that a spreadsheet program would be very helpful to them. What features should she look for in making a decision on which program to buy?

Help? See Unit 5.6 Information Bank page 69.

Extension task

During the next week make a list of those occasions on which you see calculations being done manually that could be done on a spreadsheet. Explain how you think a spreadsheet could help.

Section 1

Unit 11 Producing invoices on a spreadsheet

By the end of this unit you will be able to use a spreadsheet program to create a simple invoice.

Scenario

Now that Sarah and Richard know how to use spreadsheets, they begin to look at other ways they could use the program to improve the efficiency and accuracy of their financial records. Sarah realises that they could produce invoices on the computer, which could be enclosed with shoes being sent out to customers. She looks at one of the invoices she has been sent by a supplier (see below), and decides to use it as a model for designing one for Stars and Stripes.

US SPORTS LTD   *Invoice*

US Sports Ltd	Invoice no: 1220		Account no:	PP520
44 Elm Street	Date: 24/11/93		Order no:	516
Cincinnatti	To: Stars & Stripes Footwear			
Ohio	42 Dock Road			
USA	Liverpool			
	L4 8TG			

Model/Size	Qty	Description	Unit price	Total amount
Sonic/6	3	White/purple	16.99	50.97
			Total: $	50.97

CREDIT TERMS: 30 days from invoice date

Stars and Stripes have set their insurance charge at 2% of the total price of the shoes, and the VAT rate is 17.5%. Therefore, if they set up a spreadsheet using the appropriate formulae, they need enter only the model and price information, and the computer will do the working out for them.

Task 1 Using your computer, construct a spreadsheet that will allow them to produce customer invoices to accompany the shoes.

Help? See Unit 13 Skills Bank page 122

Unit 11: Producing invoices on a spreadsheet

Task 2   Use the spreadsheet you have created for Task 1 to create two invoices for the two sales transactions below:
   a) one pair of APS 3000 costing £49.99
       one pair of Tri-vent costing £59.99
   b) one pair of High Flier costing £29.99
       one pair of Conqueror costing £49.99

   Print out the two invoices.

   Help? See Unit 13 Skills Bank page 122

Extension task

Using your spreadsheet create the following invoices

a) Three pairs of APS 3000
    Two pairs of Tri-vent
    Four pairs of High Flier
    Two pairs of Conqueror

b) Four pairs of APS 3000
    Three pairs of Tri-vent
    One pair of High Flier
    Six pair of Conqueror

Section 1

Unit 12 Keeping financial records on a spreadsheet

By the end of this unit you will be able to use a spreadsheet program to keep simple financial records.

Scenario

Sarah and Richard are very pleased that they can now quickly and easily calculate and print out invoices for their customers. They also know that they should be able to use the program to keep a record of the money that goes in and out of the business every day.

At present, Sarah keeps track of the money in their bank account by noting down cheques and cash going in or out on their copy of their bank statement.

Her entries for the previous few days look like this:

STATEMENT

TITLE OF ACCOUNT Stars and Stripes Footwear

ACCOUNT NUMBER 05400780

Details	Date	Payments	Receipts	Balance
	1/9/93			£100
	1/9/93		£89.00	
	1/9/93		£73.00	
000776	2/9/93	£25.60		
	2/9/93		£115.00	
000777	3/9/93	£125.00		
	3/9/93		£155.00	
	3/9/93		£89.00	
	3/9/93		£66.00	
	3/9/93		£155.00	
000778	3/9/93	£125.00		
000779	4/9/93	£400.00		
	4/9/93		£102.00	

Task 1 Design and complete a spreadsheet that can calculate the balance (total) in their bank account, and enter into it the transactions above. Complete the balance column (only the first balance has been given) using a formula that will take the previous balance and add to it or take away from it as appropriate.

Help? See Units 10–13 Skills Bank page 119

Unit 12: Keeping financial records on a spreadsheet

Task 2   Enter the following items into the spreadsheet, and print out one copy:

Shoes sold to D White on 5/9/93 for £125.00

Shoes sold to F Rogers on 5/9/93 for £168.95

Shoes sold to R Christie on 5/9/93 for £75.28

Postage paid on 5/9/93 of £26.50

Shoes sold to A Heffernon on 6/9/93 for £212.64

Shoes sold to G Hendon on 6/9/93 for £75.28

Telephone bill paid on 7/9/93 for £183.76

Help? See Units 10–13 Skills Bank page 119

Extension task

Enter the following, additional, items into the spreadsheet, and print out one copy:

Shoes sold to Sport Scene on 8/9/93 for £356.75

Shoes sold to M. Williams on 8/9/93 for £87.50

Shoes sold to J. Penketh on 9/9/93 for £112.80

Shoes sold to K. Stamp on 10/9/93 for £124.75

Wages to Sarah on 10/9/93 of £125

Wages to Richard on 10/9/93 of £125

Section 1

Unit 13 Displaying information

By the end of this unit you will be able to recognise and interpret some of the different types of graph, and you will be able to produce them from your spreadsheet program.

Scenario

Sarah and Richard are due to visit their bank manager to update him on how their business is doing. They want to present him with the figures below showing sales and profits over the previous six months, and want to make their presentation as professional as possible.

Sales of different types of footwear

TYPE	SALES VALUE(£)
LEISURE	1250
FASHION	1755
SPORTING	895
SPECIALIST	2100

Profit figures (in £)

January	February	March	April	May	June
145	175	250	350	425	535

Task 1 Which kind of chart or graph do you think would be most suitable for presenting the sales figures above? Which do you think would effectively show the profit figures?

Help? See Unit 5.5 Information Bank page 67.

Task 2 Using your Spreadsheet produce a pie chart based on the above sales figures. Print your chart and save your spreadsheet.

Help? See Unit 14 Skills Bank page 123.

Task 3 Using the above profit figures, manually produce a line chart of the profit made over the six months.

Help? See Unit 5.5 Information Bank page 67.

Task 4 Using your spreadsheet produce a line chart based on the same figures. Print the chart and save your spreadsheet.

Help? See Unit 14 Skills Bank page 123.

Unit 13: Displaying information

When they check their figures before visiting the bank manager, they realise they have made a couple of mistakes. The sales value of sporting shoes should have been 1025, the profit for February should have been 157 and for June should have been 553.

Task 5   Make the above changes to your spreadsheets and print out the amended pie and line charts.

Extension Task

Collect a number of examples of graphs and charts from a variety of sources, eg newspapers, magazines and official publications. Label each one explaining what type of chart it is, what it shows and where it comes from.

Which ones do you think illustrate the information most effectively?

Section 1

Unit 14 Controlling the system

By the end of this unit you will understand what an operating system is and what part it plays in the working of a computer.

Scenario

Richard and Sarah have been researching thoroughly which computer would be the best for their needs (and their pocket) before buying one. They have already discovered that the memory capacity of the computer hardware they choose will effect what applications software they can successfully run on it (see Unit 7). A shop assistant in the computer store tells them they must also know the system software of their particular computer before choosing any application packages.

Task 1   What does the assistant mean by 'system software'?

>   **Help?** See Unit 6.1 Information Bank page 69.

When they tell the assistant what computer they are considering buying, he says 'Ah, it's a PC, and therefore runs on MSDOS'.

Task 2   What does MSDOS stand for, and how will it affect their choice of application?

>   **Help?** See Unit 6.2 Information Bank page 69.

Realising that they are both unfamiliar with computers, the assistant suggests they consider also buying *Windows* to make the application easier to use.

Task 3   What is 'Windows' and why do you think it has become so popular?

>   **Help?** See Unit 6.3 Information Bank page 70.

Extension Task

Sarah wonders how many different types of operating system there might be. Using computers at your place of study, work, home and amongst friends select two computers with different operating systems, describe what they are and how they are being used.

Unit 15 Keeping track of stock

By the end of this unit you will be able to set up a manual record-keeping system and know its limitations and disadvantages.

Scenario

Richard and Sarah need to keep accurate records of the amount of stock that they have in their store room. In order to do this they have created sets of index cards containing information about each type of footwear they sell. On each stock index card are details showing the make, model, item number, size range, colour, the number currently in stock and the retail price.

Task 1   Create a set of 20 index cards using the data shown below.

Task 2   To be useful the records need to be organised so that individual cards can be found and retrieved quickly. Sort the cards into alphabetical order by **make**.

Task 3   Make the following alterations to the stock file:

a) Stocks for the model DIAMIC 5G made by STREETLIFE have been reduced to 17.

b) A new model by PBS is now available and a new record needs to be created and inserted alphabetically into the database file.

The details are:

Item no:	PE8422
Make:	PBSMODEL: TORNADO II
Size:	3-7COLOUR: WH
No in stock:	20
Retail value:	£39.99

c) The price of CONQUEROR trainers made by LEOPARD have been reduced from £49.99 to £39.99.

Data for index cards

ITEMNO: PE7136	
MAKE: AMERICANO	MODEL: SONIC
SIZE: 6-11	COLOUR: WH/PU
NO IN STOCK: 12	RETAIL VALUE: 29.99

ITEMNO: PE7249	
MAKE: APIPCO	MODEL: GAZELLE
SIZE: 7-12	COLOUR: BL
NO IN STOCK:	RETAIL VALUE: 35.99

ITEMNO: PE7351	
MAKE: PBS	MODEL: HIGH SHOT
SIZE: 5-9	COLOUR: BL/WH
NO IN STOCK: 22	RETAIL VALUE: 49.99

ITEMNO: PE7467	
MAKE: SPX	MODEL: IMPACT
SIZE: 5-9	COLOUR: WH/BL
NO IN STOCK: 14	RETAIL VALUE: 49.99

ITEMNO: PE7589	
MAKE: PBS	MODEL: ASTRO
SIZE: 6-8	COLOUR: WH/BL
NO IN STOCK: 17	RETAIL VALUE: 49.99

ITEMNO: PE7691	
MAKE: LEOPARD	MODEL: TORTILLO
SIZE: 5-10	COLOUR: BL
NO IN STOCK: 8	RETAIL VALUE: 39.99

Section 1

ITEMNO: PE7792 MAKE: AMERICANO MODEL: APS 2000 SIZE: 6-9 COLOUR: WH/BL NO IN STOCK: 13 RETAIL VALUE: 55.99	ITEMNO: PE789 MAKE: LEOPARD MODEL: CONQUEROR SIZE: 5-8 COLOUR: WH/PU NO IN STOCK: 9 RETAIL VALUE: 49.99
ITEMNO: PE7901 MAKE: STREETLIFE MODEL: DIAMIC 5G SIZE: 6-11 COLOUR: GR/RE NO IN STOCK: 20 RETAIL VALUE: 29.99	ITEMNO: PE7904 MAKE: KOALA MODEL: PREDATOR 5 SIZE: 4-9 COLOUR: WH/BL NO IN STOCK: 6 RETAIL VALUE: 39.99
ITEMNO: PE7910I MAKE: SPX MODEL: SLAPSHOT SIZE: 4-9 COLOUR: WH/PU NO IN STOCK: 9 RETAIL VALUE: 42.99	TEMNO: PE8012 MAKE: AZTECS MODEL: TRI-VENT SIZE: 5-11 COLOUR: BLUE NO IN STOCK: 14 RETAIL VALUE: 59.99
ITEMNO: PE8115I MAKE: APIPCO MODEL: HURRICANE SIZE: 4-8 COLOUR: BL/MAG NO IN STOCK: 8 RETAIL VALUE: 49.99	TEMNO: PE8216 MAKE: PBS MODEL: TORNADO SIZE: 3-7 COLOUR: WH NO IN STOCK: 9 RETAIL VALUE: 69.99
ITEMNO: PE8220 MAKE: SPX MODEL: SUPER 9 SIZE: 4-9 COLOUR: BL/WH NO IN STOCK: 14 RETAIL VALUE: 49.99	ITEMNO: PE8224 MAKE: APIPCO MODEL: HIGH FLIER SIZE: 3-9 COLOUR: BL/GR NO IN STOCK: 12 RETAIL VALUE: 29.99
ITEMNO: PE8226 MAKE: AMERICANO MODEL: APS 3000 SIZE: 5-9 COLOUR: RE/BL NO IN STOCK: 23 RETAIL VALUE: 49.99	ITEMNO: PE8230 MAKE: LEOPARD MODEL: TRIDENT SIZE: 4-9 COLOUR: WH/BL NO IN STOCK: 14 RETAIL VALUE: 39.99
ITEMNO: PE8235 MAKE: STREETLIFE MODEL: DYNAzMO 33 SIZE: 6-11 COLOUR: PU NO IN STOCK: 10 RETAIL VALUE: 19.99	ITEMNO: PE8238 MAKE: KOALA MODEL: TERMINATOR SIZE: 4-9 COLOUR: BL/GR NO IN STOCK: 15 RETAIL VALUE: 49.99

Task 4   Many customers telephone saying they would like to buy a pair of trainers, but have only a limited amount of money to spend. Sarah and Richard need to be able to identify which ones customers could afford. Rearrange the cards into descending order of **retail value** (ie lowest priced first) so that Sarah can refer to the list of stock on a sliding scale of price.

Task 5   Richard has been receiving many enquiries regarding specific models of trainer and feels it would better if the cards were organised into alphabetical order by **model**. Rearrange the index cards accordingly.

Extension task

Richard wants to look at the cards arranged in ascending order of stock level so that he can see at a glance of which model he has the most stock. Rearrange the cards into ascending order of number in stock.

Unit 16 Computerising the stock records

By the end of this unit you will be familiar with computerised record-keeping systems, and know how to create a simple database file.

Scenario

Richard and Sarah agree that the manual record-keeping system needs replacing because it cannot quickly and easily give them the information they need about the shoes in stock. Therefore, they decide to put all the data onto a computerised database file.

Task 1   What is a database?

Help? See Unit 8.1 Information Bank page 74.

Task 2   In order to create the database Richard and Sarah need to specify the number and type of items of data (or fields) needed for the computer records. Why are fields important in creating records?

Help? See Unit 8.2 Information Bank page 74.

Task 3   Using your computer, create a database file, enter the data from the index cards into this database file and save it.

Help? See Unit 15 Skills Bank page 129.

Section 1

Unit 17 Amending the database

By the end of this unit you will be able to edit and manipulate data on an existing database file to produce a variety of reports or lists.

Scenario

Having entered all the data from the index cards on to the computer, Richard and Sarah find their handling of stock is much improved. They now find that they can more easily provide different views of the information to help answer customer enquiries.

Task 1   The records need to be reorganised so that the data can be found and retrieved quickly. Organise the records into alphabetical order by **make**. Print a report of the data stored on the computer. Re-save your file.

Help? See Units 16 and 17 Skills Bank page 131.

Task 2   After the file has been set up, Richard realises there are some changes which need to be made:

a) stocks for the model Diamic 5G, which is made by STREETLIFE, have been reduced to 13;

b) a new model called WHITESTORM by APIPCO is now available, and a new record needs to be set up (the item number is PE8245, it is available in white and black, there are 20 in stock in sizes 6-12). The new record should be inserted alphabetically into the database file.

c) the price of CONQUEROR trainers made by LEOPARD have been reduced again from £39.99 to £29.99.

Make these changes, print out a report and re-save your file.

Help? See Units 16 and 17 Skills Bank page 131.

Task 3   To answer the queries of those customers who have a limited amount of money to spend on trainers, rearrange the database file into descending order of retail value. Print a report.

Help? See Units 16 and 17 Skills Bank page 131.

Extension task

Richard wants to look at the records in ascending order of stock numbers so that he can see easily of which model he has the most stock. Rearrange the file into ascending order of number in stock.

Unit 18 Interrogating the database

By the end of this unit you will be able to use a database to answer more detailed queries about the data held on it.

Scenario

Now that he has replaced the manual record-keeping system with the computerised database, Richard can answer very specific customer queries about the trainers they sell.

Task 1   A customer has requested information on all the footwear made by Americano. Interrogate the database file to search for this information and print a report showing the result of your search.

Help? See Unit 18 Skills Bank page 134.

Task 2   Another customer rings who does not wish to pay more than £40.00 for a pair of shoes. Interrogate the database file and print a report showing only those shoes below £40.00.

Help? See Unit 18 Skills Bank page 134.

Task 3   Another customer wants to know which shoes by PBS he could buy for under £50.00. Print a report which Richard could send to him showing which shoes he could buy.

Help? See Unit 18 Skills Bank page 134

Task 4   Which of the following customer queries require sorting and which require selecting:

a) a list of all footwear organised in alphabetical order by make

b) a list of footwear made by Apipco

c) a list of footwear arranged by price showing the most expensive first

Help? See Unit 8.3 Information Bank page 75.

Extension task 1

Richard needs to find out which shoes have low stock levels so that he can order some more. Interrogate the database file and print a report which shows stock items whose levels are under 10.

Extension task 2

Richard is thinking of offering some price reductions on those shoes of which there are 10 or more pairs in stock, and whose prices lie in the £20.00 to £40.00 price range. Print a report of those shoes which satisfy these criteria.

Section 1

Unit 19 Using a database appropriately and effectively

By the end of this unit you will appreciate the benefits and the other applications of computer database systems, and you will be aware of the legal restrictions on their use.

Scenario

The database system seems to be helping considerably with answering customer queries on prices and availability, and is making stock control more efficient.

Richard and Sarah are so impressed with their database system that they try and think of any other area of the business that it could improve.

Task 1   What are some of the other benefits of the computerised system to Stars and Stripes?

   Help? See Unit 8.3 Information Bank page 75.

Task 2   Looking back at the order processing procedures on page 4 identify one other task that could be completed more efficiently if it moved onto the computerised database system.

   Help? See Unit 8.3 Information Bank page 75.

Task 3   Once Richard and Sarah have put all their financial and stock records on computer, what legislation should they be aware of regarding the computerised data?

   Help? See Unit 8.4 Information Bank page 77.

Task 4   Which businesses or services do you think would need to be particularly aware of this legislation, and why might members of the public want to exercise the rights it gives them?

   Help? See Unit 8.4 Information Bank page 77.

Extension Task

Using your place of work or study as an example examine how well the word processor, database and spreadsheet you have used have met your needs, particularly in the areas of:

a) ease of use and learning

b) range of facilities – highlighting which you feel are most useful

c) possible improvements that you feel there could be.

Unit 20 Hard disks and other data storage media

By the end of this unit you will know the advantages of using a hard disk and some of the other media for storing data.

Scenario

Both Richard and Sarah are finding that continually loading their computer with database, spreadsheet and word processing programs from a floppy disk, and then having to load the data separately from another floppy disk, is very time consuming. Their friend Rebecca suggests that they upgrade their computer by connecting it to a hard disk.

Task 1   Explain what a hard disk is, its advantages over a floppy disk system and why it might be more useful to Stars and Stripes.

Help? See Unit 9.1 Information Bank page 78.

Task 2   What simple precaution should they take to protect data on the hard disk from being lost?

Help? See Unit 9.1 Information Bank page 78.

Task 3   Richard has heard of other data storage systems such as CD-ROM, optical disks, magneto-optical disks and magnetic tapes. Explain where these are used and if they would be of any help to Richard and Sarah.

Help? See Unit 9.2–9.4 Information Bank page 78.

Extension task

Looking at your place of study/work, produce a list of the different types of storage systems available, with sizes, and state what they are used for.

Section 1

Unit 21 Staying secure

By the end of this unit you will know how to avoid losing the data on your computer and how to keep it secure. You will also be aware of health and safety considerations.

Scenario

One day Richard switches on the computer and is greeted by a systems crash message. Knowing that all the company's financial and stock information and correspondence was held on the hard disk, Richard panics, and regrets having put all the company's most vital information in one storage system. Fortunately, the computer works as normal when he makes a second attempt to switch it on, but the incident serves to teach him how vital it is to the business that the information on computer is not lost, and he decides to find out how to make it more secure.

Task 1   What do you think are the main risks to the data stored on Richard's and Sarah's computer? What other risks are there that could be a factor in other companies and situations?

Help? See Unit 10.1 Information Bank page 80.

Task 2   What physical and software security measures could they employ to protect the data stored on their computer? What methods could be used to protect against the other risks you gave in Task 1?

Help? See Unit 10.2 and 10.3 Information Bank page 80.

Task 3   If Richard had lost all the information on the computer through a systems crash, what simple *administrative* procedures would have helped to minimise the effects of the loss?

Help? See Unit 10.4 Information Bank page 82.

One day Sarah is given some ideas for advertisement design on a floppy disk by her friend Rebecca. Soon after she accesses the disk, her computer starts behaving unpredictably and she finds she cannot access other files on her hard disk.

Task 4   What is likely to have affected her computer? How could this have happened and how could Sarah have avoided it?

Help? See Unit 10.5 Information Bank page 82.

Now that they are using their computer regularly, Richard and Sarah need to set it up so that it is as safe and comfortable to use as possible.

Task 5   Draw up a checklist of points they should consider when designing a suitable workstation for their computer.

Help? See Unit 10.6 Information Bank page 83.

Extension task

Assess your own workstation at work, home or college and list those features you think should be improved to meet health and safety guidelines.

Unit 22 Producing letterheads and logos

By the end of this unit you will be able to use computer graphics in the design and creation of documents.

Scenario

When they had first started the business, Richard and Sarah had some headed paper (see Unit 2 page 6) designed (at considerable expense) and printed which now needs some alterations to include their VAT number and telephone number. They decide to redesign their logo at the same time, but want to save money on the design and artwork by producing it themselves using a graphics package on their computer.

Task 1   They are unsure of the differences between a paint package and a draw package. Explain the differences, and which one would be most suitable for them.

   Help? See Unit 11.1 Information Bank page 84.

Task 2   Using a graphics package on your computer design a suitable logo for Stars and Stripes Footwear which can be used on their headed paper and business cards.

   Help? See Units 19–23 Skills Bank page 138.

Task 3   Richard is not very confident about his artistic ability when creating a logo. What supporting software is available that could help him?

   Help? See Unit 11.2 Information Bank page 87.

Extension task

Richard is thinking of putting a small advertisement (10cm x 20cm) in their local paper. Using a graphics package on your computer, design an advertisement that will promote the company and the footwear it sells by mail order.

Section 1

Unit 23 Page layout

By the end of this unit you will have some knowledge of what desktop publishing involves and how it can be used.

Scenario

Richard and Sarah wish to produce a sales brochure that will contain details of their products, including pictures and price lists.

Task 1   How could they produce an impressive brochure themselves, ready for the printers, without needing to employ an expensive designer?

Help? See Unit 12.1 and 12.2 Information Bank page 87.

Task 2   What type of package do you think would be most suitable for Stars and Stripes, and why?

Help? See Unit 12.3 Information Bank page 88.

Task 3   Using your computer, produce a one page sheet publicising Stars and Stripes Footwear. It should include a headline, some graphics and two columns of text.

Task 4   Using your place of work or study as an example examine how well your desktop publishing program meets your needs particularly in the areas of:

a) ease of use and learning

b) range of facilities – highlighting which you feel are most useful

c) possible improvements that you feel there could be

Help? See Units 7.2 and 12 Information Bank pages 72 and 87.

Extension Task

Collect and then compare three different publications. Look at the number of columns, the number and type of illustrations, the size and shape of the text and any other features you feel are important. As a result of your analysis, decide which publication is the most appealing to read and why.

Unit 24 Running complex programs

By the end of this unit you will understand what is required to use more complex programs.

Scenario

Now Richard and Sarah have seen how graphics and desktop publishing can enhance advertisements and leaflets, they enquire about buying their own package. They are told however, that their computer does not have a powerful enough microprocessor or a good enough monitor to run this type of program well.

Task 1 Suggest two microprocessors that would be suitable for running graphics and desktop publishing programs

Help? See Unit 4.4 Information Bank page 59.

Task 2 They have been advised that they need a monitor with a higher resolution. Explain what this means and suggest two grades of monitor that might be suitable.

Help? See Unit 4.5 Information Bank page 61.

Extension Task

Using computers at your place of study, work, home and amongst friends, select four different computers, describe what microprocessor(s) they contain and what they are used for.

Section 1

Unit 25 Saving time

By the end of this unit you will know which devices are used to input data for different purposes.

Scenario

Sarah wants to investigate the possibility of reducing the amount of keyboard work that she and Richard do every time stock arrives at or leaves the warehouse.

Data relating to the make, model, colour, size and description of the shoes has to be entered into the computer in order to keep accurate records, and this is a time-consuming process. Sarah was thinking of purchasing a bar code reader since all the boxes arrive from America with bar code labels stuck to them.

Task 1 Give a brief explanation of a how a bar code system works and what information it could input to their computer.

Help? See Unit 13.1 Information Bank page 90.

Task 2 In a magazine, Sarah searches for alternative input devices to a keyboard and finds the following:

a) light pen
b) kimball tag reader
c) magnetic ink character reader
d) optical character reader
e) optical mark reader
f) mouse
g) scanner

Would any of these be suitable for her purpose, and if not, where do you think they would be useful?

Help? See Unit 13.2 and 13.3 Information Bank page 91.

Extension task

If Sarah decides they cannot afford to purchase a bar code reader she will enrole on a course to improve her keyboard skills. When she looks at the keyboard she is puzzled by all the extra keys that exist in addition to the numerical and alphabetical keys. Look at the extra keys on your keyboard and investigate their purpose and add them to your system notes.

Unit 26 Going into print

By the end of this unit you will be familiar with the different printing devices that can be used with computers.

Scenario

When Richard and Sarah first borrowed their computer they were also lent a small printer, called a dot matrix printer, which they have been using for printing out stock lists, spreadsheet calculations and letters to customers and suppliers.

Though they are happy with the reliability of the printer, the quality of print is not very good, especially for letters to potential customers. They both feel that the image of the business is important and that they need to replace their existing printer with something better.

Task 1 What do you think the advantages and disadvantages of dot matrix, inkjet and laser printers would be to Richard and Sarah? Include how each printer works in your answer.

Help? See Unit 14.1 – 14.3 Information Bank page 92.

Task 2 Word process a list of five possible models of each of the types of printer that Richard and Sarah could buy. Use up-to-date computer magazines to help you with your answer.

Task 3 Richard and Sarah wonder what the cost of producing a single A4 sheet of text is. Basing your investigations on the printer you are currently using, find out and calculate how much it costs to print one sheet of text on A4 paper taking into account, in addition to the cost of paper, the cost of ribbons or toner cartridges. You also need to find out how many copies can be printed from one ribbon or cartridge before it needs to be replaced

Extension task

Collect some examples of printed output from the three types of printer mentioned and compare the quality of output. Make a list of jobs each would be most suited to tackle.

Section 1

Unit 27 Keeping in touch

By the end of this unit you will know which of the various communication technology devices is suitable for which purpose.

Scenario

Richard returns to the office one afternoon and an exasperated Sarah explains that she has been trying to contact him for hours because a vital order has gone missing. Richard alone knows the details as he had placed the order by telephone with one of their American suppliers. He immediately phones the supplier in New York, but only succeeds in reaching an answering service.

They decide that they must look into ways of improving their communication systems as one or other of them is frequently away from the office and their business relies on quick decisions.

Task 1 Much of their business is done over the telephone, and they are considering replacing their telephone with a more sophisticated system. What features do you think they should look for?

Help? See Unit 15.1 and 15.2 Information Bank page 94.

Task 2 Do you think a cellular telephone could ensure this situation doesn't arise again? Explain your answer.

Help? See Unit 15.3 Information Bank page 95.

Task 3 Delay in contacting customers and suppliers can cause considerable commercial and financial damage to an organisation. What faster and more convenient alternatives to the postal service are available for businesses?

Help? See Unit 15.4 Information Bank page 95.

Extension task

Make a list of advantages to a business of having an electronic mailbox in which messages can be left.

Unit 28 On-line

By the end of this unit you will know the benefits of an on-line database to many businesses.

Scenario

Richard needs to go to New York urgently to resolve some problems with a particular supplier. He needs to know when the next flight to New York leaves Manchester airport, but when he rings the flight information desk, he keeps getting the engaged tone. Eventually he gets through, discovers the plane is to leave in two hours, and drives to the airport as fast as he can. Much to his annoyance, he is held up in a five mile traffic jam on the M56 and misses the plane.

Task 1 Richard's delay in contacting the flight information desk, and his hold-up in a severe traffic jam could both have been avoided if he had had access to an on-line database holding up-to-date travel information. What is an on-line database, and which businesses do you think would benefit most from having access to one?

Help? See Unit 15.5 Information Bank page 97.

Task 2 What is a bulletin board in terms of electronic communication?

Help? See Unit 15.5 Information Bank page 97.

Task 3 What is the difference between Viewdata and Teletext systems?

Help? See Unit 15.6 Information Bank page 97.

Extension task

Find out and make a list of the sort of information that can be found on Teletext systems.

Section 1

Unit 29 Extending expertise

By the end of this unit you will know of other software applications and when they might be used.

Scenario

Sarah and Richard are very pleased with the different types of uses to which they have put their computer, but wonder if there may be other useful applications available to them.

Richard has enjoyed using the word processor, database and spreadsheet but knows that sometimes it would be useful to put some or all of the output together in one document such as a brochure or an annual report.

Task 1 Look back at the list of tasks in their order processing procedures (page 4). Which time consuming and routine operations could be accomplished better on computer?

Help? See Unit 16 Information Bank page 99.

Task 2 Explain to Richard what types of program can incorporate all of the above applications easily. Highlight for him any advantages of this sort of program, and any possible problems to be aware of. Suggest some packages he might like to consider.

Help? See Section 2 Units 17.1 and 17.2 Information Bank page 99.

Extension Task

Richard has seen MIDI referred to in several information technology magazines, and has been wondering what it is and if it would be useful to Stars and Stripes. Explain to Richard what MIDI is, whether it would be useful to Stars and Stripes, and what types of equipment would be required to start using it.

Help? See Unit 18 Information Bank page 101.

Unit 30 Information technology applications

By the end of this unit you should have a better understanding of how information technology can be applied to information processing activities.

Scenario Epilogue

Richard and Sarah began their business venture with little knowledge and experience of information technology. However, they both now feel confident that they can use information technology to help solve many business problems and manage the business more efficiently. They are sufficiently well equipped to take a wider view of their business and to consider which information technology devices would be of use to them in performing their daily business routines.

Task 1 Referring to the table that you completed in Unit 1 page 5, complete the table below, indicating the information devices you think could help them at each of the four stages of processing information when tackling their daily routine.

Help? See Unit 1.3 Information Bank page 48.

Answer in appendix page 158.

Job	IT device for capture	IT device for process retrieval	IT device for storage	IT device for communication
Receive Order	Keyboard Fax machine OCR, OMR	Computer system running database application software	Computer with hard disk, magnetic disk, magnetic tape or optical disk	Telephone or fax if required to communicate quickly with customer. Printer linked to computer to print lists. VDU screen for display

Extension task

Information technology has had an impact on every aspect of our society. Investigate one aspect and prepare a short presentation.

Help? See Unit 19.1–19.8 Information Bank page 102.

Section 2 Information bank

This section contains all the necessary information to enable you to answer the tasks in Section 1. It is not intended to be read from beginning to end, but should be read as directed from Section 1.

Contents

Unit 1 Information technology 46
Unit 2 Word processing 49
Unit 3 Floppy disk backing storage 54
Unit 4 Computer hardware 56
Unit 5 Spreadsheets 64
Unit 6 Systems software 69
Unit 7 Application software 71
Unit 8 Databases 74
Unit 9 Hard disks and other backing storage media 78
Unit 10 Data security and safety 80
Unit 11 Computer graphics 84
Unit 12 Desktop publishing 87
Unit 13 Input devices 90
Unit 14 Output devices – printers 92
Unit 15 Communications technology 94
Unit 16 Accounting/Bookkeeping packages 99
Unit 17 Integrated software 99
Unit 18 Musical instrument digital interface 101
Unit 19 Information technology applications 102

Unit 1 Information technology

1.1 What is information?

Information is data (the raw material of information) that has been processed in some way. It appears in three main forms.

Numeric data: quantities, prices, telephone numbers, measurements of time, distance, speed, weight, height, age etc.

Alphabetic data: names, description of goods, business letters etc.

(A combination of numeric and alphabetic data, eg an address with a house number and a road name is called *alphanumeric* data)

Graphic data: business charts and graphic images.

These different types of data may appear independently or more usually in combination with one other. For example, a business quotation will contain a description of goods (alphabetical data), the name and address of the firm giving the quotation (alphanumeric data), the telephone and fax numbers of the firm (numeric data), together with the prices of the goods (numeric data).

In a business organisation the data processed would concern all of the business's activities, for example customer and supplier orders and invoices, income generated from sales, money spent on electricity, heat, lighting and wage bills. In fact, every business transaction or activity that takes place involves the processing of data. How this data is collected and processed into information, stored and communicated, is the study of information processing.

1.2 Information Processing

The processing of data into information can be divided into four distinct activities:

- **Data capture**

Data can be collected through observation, written documentation, reference to graphs or charts, through the physical activity of measuring and recording or verbally through interviews and conversations. See the diagram on the following page.

- **Processing the data**

Once the data has been gathered it needs to be processed. It is this activity of processing that distinguishes data from information. Data consists of meaningless numbers and letters and it is the processing activity that transforms the data into meaningful information. This might embrace such activities as sorting, comparing, editing, calculating, moving or coding data. The result of these activities is to produce meaningful information that can be understood and used by the recipient.

- **Storing and retrieving the information**

Once processed, all valuable and useful information needs to be stored logically and kept in a place which is readily accessible so that there is no difficulty in locating and retrieving the information when necessary.

- **Communicating the information**

The value of information lies in its contribution to helping an individual or an organisation meet its objectives. Information, therefore, needs to be shared and used by members of the

Unit 1: Information technology

organisation. Communicating information involves both verbal and non-verbal methods (see the diagram below)

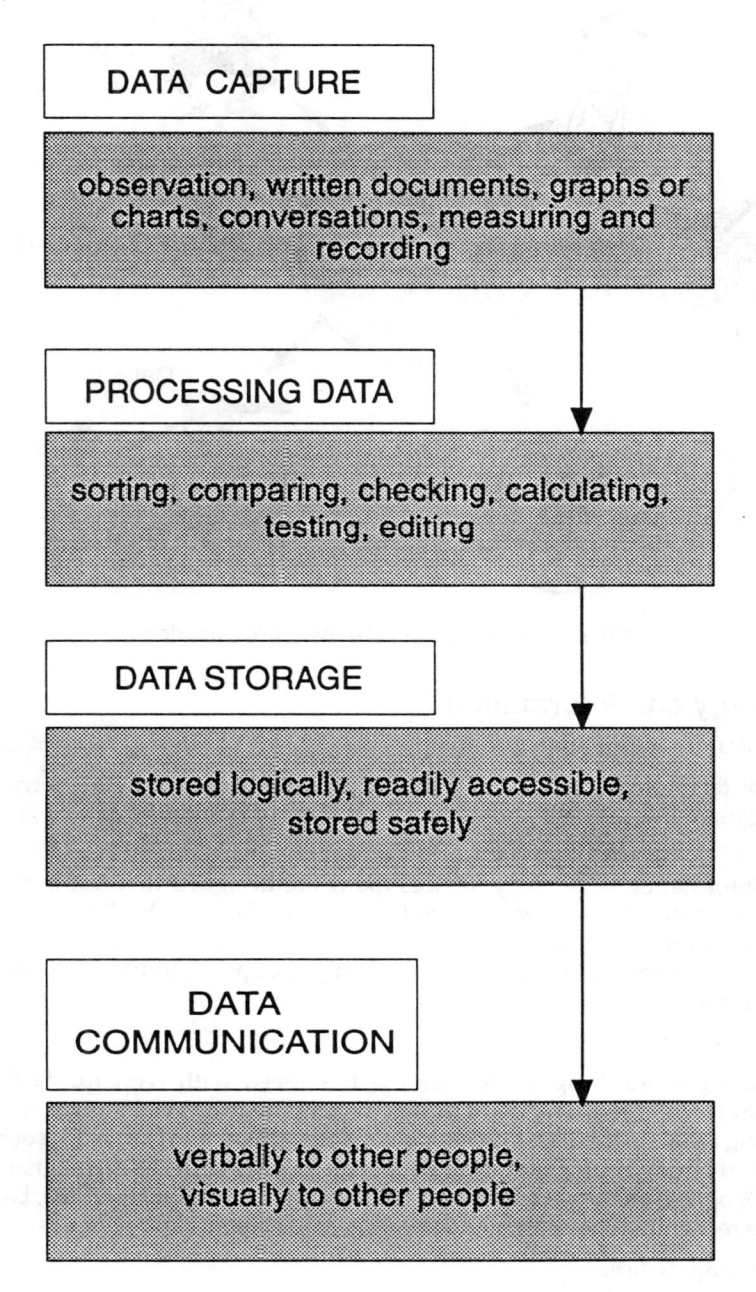

DATA CAPTURE

observation, written documents, graphs or charts, conversations, measuring and recording

PROCESSING DATA

sorting, comparing, checking, calculating, testing, editing

DATA STORAGE

stored logically, readily accessible, stored safely

DATA COMMUNICATION

verbally to other people, visually to other people

The four stages of information processing

Section 2

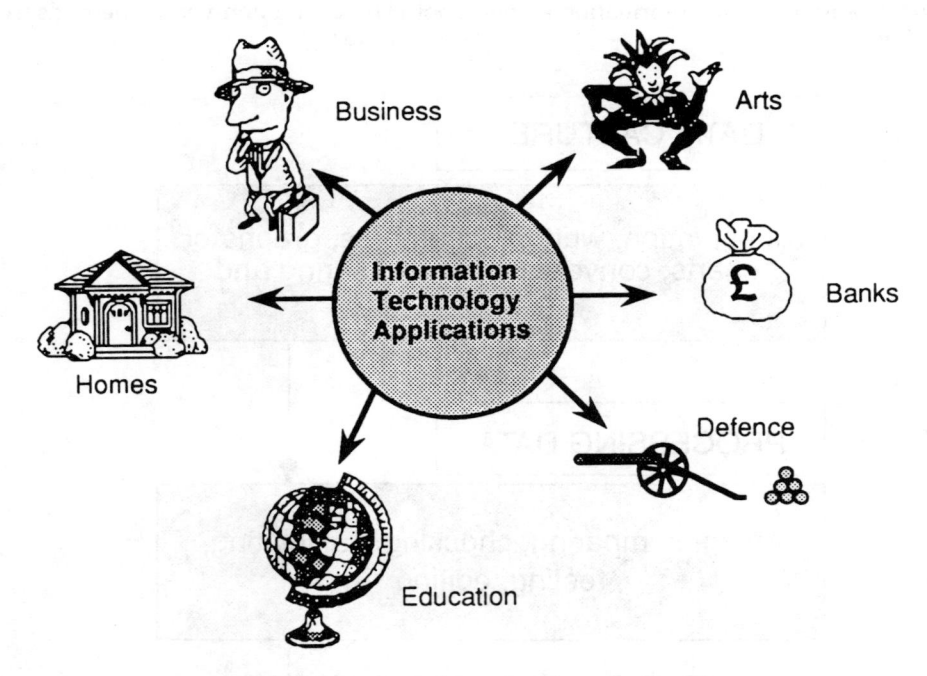

Different information technology applications

1.3 Technology and information

The dictionary defines information technology as:

> 'the use of technology to aid the capture, processing, storage and retrieval, and communication of information whether in the form of numerical data, text, image or sound.'

Most modern information technology devices today are designed to assist in the processing of information as it passes through each of its four stages. They are built to improve speed and efficiency in the way that information is handled, replacing slower manual practises with faster new technological methods. They can be conveniently grouped into the following four stages of processing information.

☐ **Data capture devices**

Data capture devices are designed to increase the speed with which data flowing into an organisation can be collected. The trend in this development has been to reduce the amount of paper and keying in by operators by developing devices that are able to read 'source' documents instantly. Modern IT devices for capturing data include keyboards, mice, magnetic ink character readers (MICR), optical character readers (OCR), optical mark readers (OMR), bar code readers, digitisers, voice recognition devices, microphones, video cameras and scanners.

☐ **Data processing devices**

The devices that actually process the data into information are not obvious and the type of device used for processing information very much depends upon on what form the information takes. Data, for example, inputted into a computer is processed by microprocessors, whereas sound in a recording studio is processed by a music mixer, telephone calls are processed by message switching devices and photographic film is processed into colour images.

Unit 1: Information technology

☐ **Storage devices**

Storage devices have developed rapidly in the last ten years, with devices becoming physically smaller and cheaper to buy but with increased storage capacity. In the early eighties hard disks with storage capacities of 10 Mb were considered more than adequate for business needs and were extremely expensive. By today's standards 10 Mb is not adequate, and upwards of 80 Mb is not only advisable but also affordable. Optical disks have capacities of over 600 Mb! Storage devices include magnetic tape, floppy disks, optical disks (CD-ROM, WORM) and memory chips.

☐ **Communication devices**

The development of communication devices has resulted in instant communication being easily possible between people in different parts of the globe. For all types of organisations this has meant an increase in efficiency and an improvement in the distribution of information both within and outside the organisation. Communication devices range from simple devices like visual display units (VDU), printers and plotters, to more sophisticated telecommunication devices like telephones, facsimile machines and telex terminals.

Unit 2 Word processing

2.1 Introduction

The first computers were designed to work with numbers, but it wasn't long before computer designers realised they could also be used for working with text. All that was required was to instruct the computer to allocate a code to each letter of the alphabet, each punctuation mark, each number and any other symbol that was to be used. As a result, when text is entered into a word processor it is converted into codes and stored in the computer's memory. This allows it to be stored on disk, recalled, worked on again and printed out as many times as is required.

2.2 Text Presentation

Working on text stored in the computer's memory has many advantages over a typewriter for producing text documents (eg a memo, a letter, report or a book):

a) when text is typed into a word processor it is stored in the memory of the computer. When the words being typed fill up the line a new line is started automatically – there is no need to press the return key. This feature is called *wordwrap*.

b) if an error does occur it is easily changed by *deleting* the error and correcting it. With a typewriter the document would have to be re-typed. If you wish to delete or add a word, *wordwrap* will automatically reposition the text to fill up the resulting space or make room for the new text.

c) it is easy to instruct the computer to alter the spaces between words so that all lines are always the same length. Thus it is possible to have the right hand side of a document *justified* so that the last characters on each line are directly under each other. It is also possible to have the text arranged so that the right side is ragged, or to have the text positioned in the centre of a line (*centred*). This positioning of text is known as *alignment*.

Section 2

2.3 Text Enhancements

A word processor allows you to clarify or emphasise text in various ways. The most frequently used are **bold** (characters are thicker), *italic* (characters slope to the right) and underlining. These effects are achieved by the computer passing instructions to the printer.

BOLD TEXT

UNDERLINE TEXT

ITALIC TEXT

SHADOW TEXT

OUTLINE TEXT

Examples of different text enhancements

2.4 Reordering Text

Since changes are carried out within the computer's memory, it is straightforward to move a large amount of text and place it in a different part of the document. It is also easy to copy portions of the text, avoiding having to re-type. All that is required is to instruct the computer which text is to be moved and where it is to be moved to. If text is to be *removed* from one place it is called *cutting*, and placing it in the new position is called *pasting*. If text is to be *repeated* elsewhere then it is termed *copying* and *pasting*.

It is also easy to make changes to individual words or phrases. Most word processors allow for a document to be *searched* for a particular word or words and, once found, they can be *changed* or *replaced*. Often this operation can be accomplished throughout a document with one instruction. The time savings can be tremendous. When *Gone With the Wind* was about to be published the heroine's name was changed from Pansy to Scarlett. Some poor individual then had to go through the entire book doggedly changing every occurrence of Pansy to Scarlett! A word processor could now accomplish a task of days within minutes. These facilities mean that editing a document with a word processor is much easier and quicker than with a typewriter.

2.5 Text Layout

Once the text has been keyed in, and any changes made, you can arrange the text on the page in a much more sophisticated way than a typewriter could manage. This is referred to as *formatting* the text. You can align text directly underneath a set point using the *tabulation* feature. It is possible to have a number of tabs set, and this makes the drawing up of tables much simpler.

However, many word processors offer additional tabulation features. A left tab will align the left-hand side of text directly under it. A right tab will align the right-hand side of text directly under it. A centre tab will centre text on the chosen point and a decimal tab will always align the decimal points directly under each other, like so:

```
        14.95
       142.95
        12.10
       123.1345
```

This is essential when presenting financial documents.

By setting the appropriate tabs at the chosen positions the drawing up of tables, containing text and/or numbers is much easier.

Most word processors make altering the right or left margins straightforward, and also more flexible, since it is possible to have *different* margin settings for different paragraphs, or even for the first lines of paragraphs. These facilities all speed up the entering of text and improve the presentation of the final document.

2.6 Additional Features

In addition to these features most word processors also take advantage of the processing speed of the computer to offer facilities way beyond anything that a traditional typewriter could provide.

Many word processors now include facilities for checking spelling, counting words and even contain *thesaurus* facilities. It is also possible to buy programs that, in conjunction with a word processor, will check grammar, meaning, writing style and readability!

10 point text

12 point text

14 point text

18 point text

24 point text

Examples of different text sizes

Many word processors also contain some drawing facilities, can include pictures in documents and can produce text in columns. Most also allow for different styles of print, or typefaces, to be used and also allow the typefaces to be used in different sizes. In addition some word processors allow the operator to store a number of commands in the memory that can be accessed by just a single keystroke; these are called *macros*. They might allow, for instance, the margin settings, line spacing and size of text for a document to be set by one keypress.

An increasingly important feature to many users is *mailmerge*, which is the ability a word processor may have to place lists of information, such as names, addresses and account details (which might be obtained from a database), into a standard form letter. This is a very useful feature since, if a standard letter needs to be sent to a great number of people, only one letter needs to be prepared and the word processor will print the number of letters required, inserting the relevant details in the correct place.

Section 2

```
Courier typeface
Geneva typeface
Monaco typeface
New York typeface
Times typeface
```

Examples of different typefaces

Many word processors are now WYSIWYG (What You See Is What You Get), which means that the printed document will look very similar, or identical, to how it looks on screen. This means that all text enhancements (such as bold or italic) and text formatting (such as columns and justification) will appear on the screen.

In addition to all of the above features, word processors can offer the following facilities which can be of use, the ability:

- to insert a header at the top of a page or a footer at a bottom of the page,
- to have pages numbered automatically and/or the time/date entered automatically,
- to assemble an index automatically,
- to import data from other programs or to export data to other programs.

The importance of any particular feature will depend upon what the word processor is to be used for.

2.7 Choosing a word processor

- **Types of word processor**

There are two main types of word processor. One, a *dedicated* word processor, is a computer that is designed specifically for word processing. It will have special keys that are used to carry out certain word processing functions. The other, and more common type, is a word processing program that can be run on a computer that is used for running other programs as well.

When purchasing a word processor the first decision to be made is whether a dedicated word processor is required, or a word processing program to run on a computer that will run other programs as well. A dedicated word processor may well be cheaper than the cost of a computer and word processing program and it might be easier to learn how to use. However, a computer running a word processing program offers much more flexibility and will probably not become obsolete so quickly, so it may well be better value in the long run. There are a large number of dedicated word processors made by a variety of manufacturers, including Amstrad, Panasonic and Brother.

Unit 2: Word processing

Dedicated word processor

Most software producers sell at least one word processing program and some sell more than one, so there are many programs to choose from. Well-known programs include Wordstar, Microsoft Word, Word for Windows, Ami Pro, Protext, WordPerfect, WordPerfect for Windows and Locoscript PC.

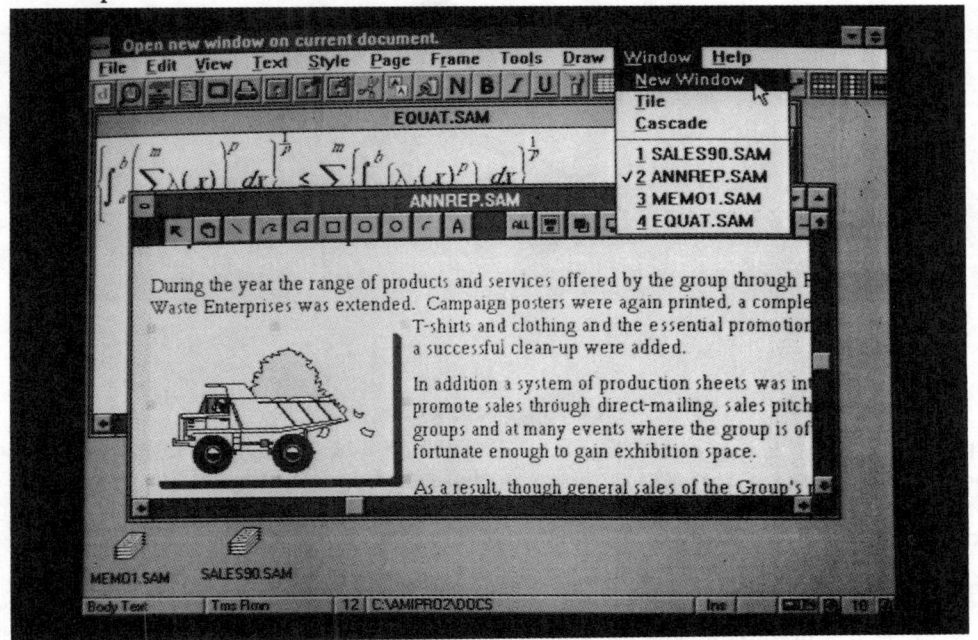

Screen from the word processing package Ami pro

Section 2

There are various features to look out for, including:

a) whether the program is WYSIWYG
b) whether it has a facility to check spelling
c) whether the word processor provides 'macros' to store your command sequences
d) whether it has a drawing facility
e) whether it allows for formatting text into columns
f) whether it is possible to import and export data to and from other programs
h) whether graphics can be incorporated into documents

Unit 3 Floppy disk backing storage

3.1 Introduction

A floppy disk is an inexpensive and portable means of holding data to be processed in a computer. There are two main sizes of floppy disk, $5^1/_4$ inch and $3^1/_2$ inch, and which one you require depends on the type of computer you are using.

A 3½ inch floppy disk

The floppy disk itself is a circular piece of plastic coated with a magnetised material which is enclosed inside a case, a soft one on $5^1/_4$ inch disks and a rigid one on $3^1/_2$ inch disks. It is important to remember that even though the outer case may be rigid the disk of magnetic material inside is still floppy.

The disk needs to be inserted into a disk drive unit (usually a slot at the front of the computer) in order that data can be stored and retrieved from its surface. Transference of data is performed by read/write heads, mounted inside the unit, moving back and forth across the disk which spins at approximately 300 revolutions per minute.

Unit 3: Floppy disk backing storage

3.2 Formatting and initialisation

Before any information can be stored on the disk it has to be prepared so that the disk drive can read the information on it and the computer can understand it. This process of preparation is called *formatting* or *initialisation*. What actually happens is that the computer divides the disk into sectors and tracks. Once the magnetic material of the disk has been arranged in this way, whenever information is stored on the disk, the computer records which track and sector it is stored in and can therefore find it again easily. Formatting a disk is similar to painting lines on a car park, the lines guide cars into an orderly arrangement and help owners return exactly to where they left their car.

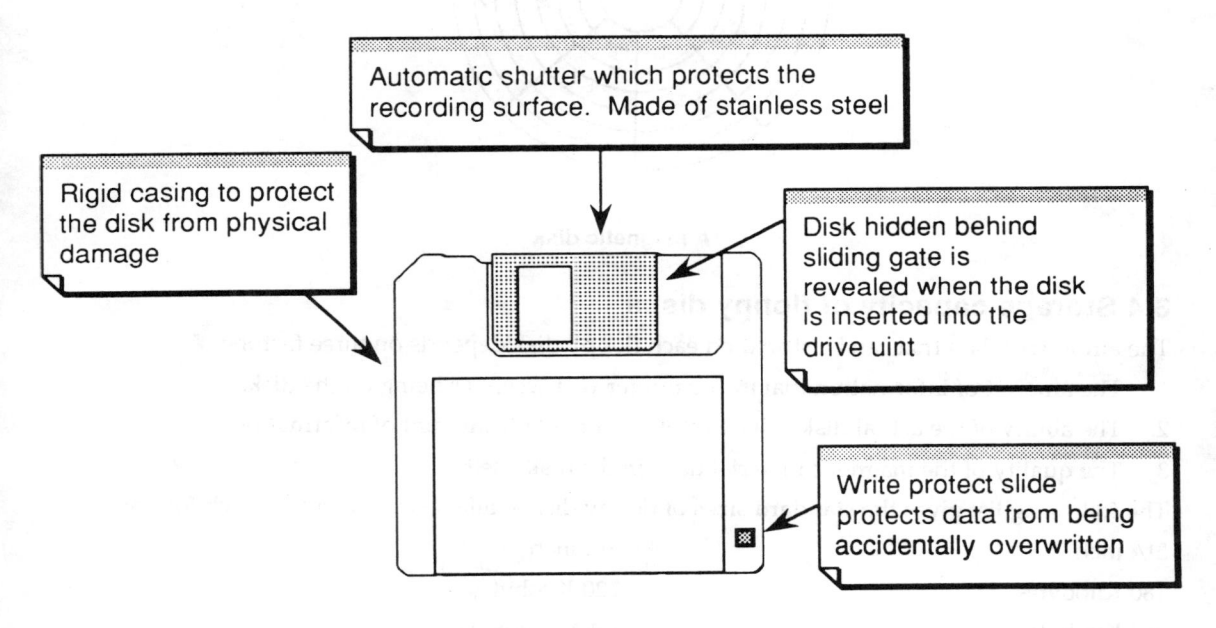

Automatic shutter which protects the recording surface. Made of stainless steel

Rigid casing to protect the disk from physical damage

Disk hidden behind sliding gate is revealed when the disk is inserted into the drive uint

Write protect slide protects data from being accidentally overwritten

The main features of a 3.5" floppy disk

3.3 The file address track

The record of where each piece of information, or file, is located is kept in the File Address Track, otherwise known as the FAT. The file address track is therefore the most important track on the disk, as without it the information on the disk could not be recalled. It is also the FAT which ensures that, when new information is placed on the disk, it does not wipe out other information that is already in place on the disk.

Section 2

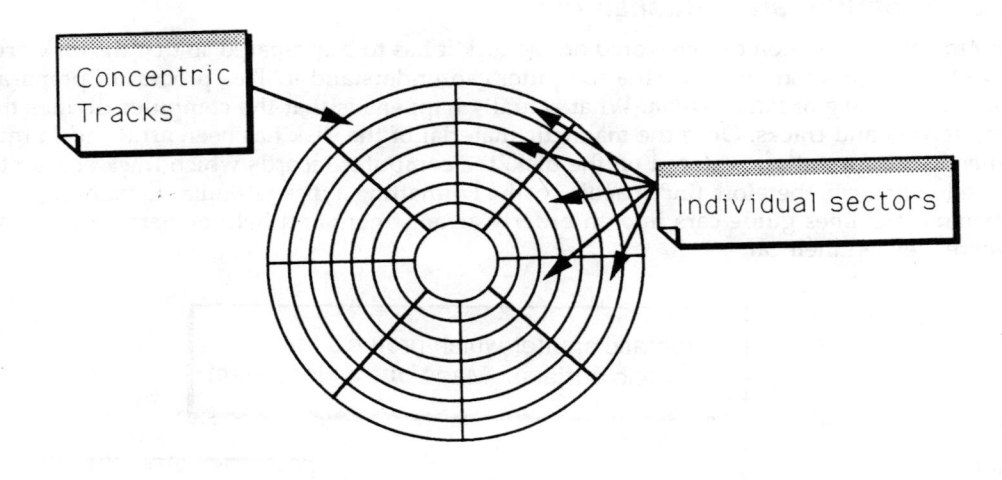

A magnetic disk

(Concentric Tracks; Individual sectors)

3.4 Storage capacity of floppy disks

The amount of data that can be stored on each floppy disk depends on three factors:

1. The amount of information that the computer will accept as being on the disk.
2. The ability of the actual disk drive to store and read the amount of information.
3. The quality of the magnetic material used in the disk itself.

The following list gives the standard sizes of floppy disk available in $5^{1}/_{4}$ and $3^{1}/_{2}$ inch format.

$5^{1}/_{4}$ inch	$3^{1}/_{2}$ inch
180 Kilobytes	720 Kilobytes
360 Kilobytes	1.4 Megabytes
720 Kilobytes	2.8 Megabytes
1.4 Megabytes	

Computer or disk memory is measured in kilobytes (kb) or megabytes (Mb). A kilobyte is approximately a thousand bytes and a megabyte a million bytes. A single byte is the amount of memory required to store a single character.

Floppy disks need to be stored carefully. They should be kept out of direct sunlight, kept at an even room temperature, always kept dry and never placed near magnetic currents. Failure to comply with these conditions may result in the data becoming corrupted and possibly lost.

Unit 4 Computer hardware

4.1 Introduction

Hardware is the name given to the actual physical components of the computer system itself, ie the computer, monitor, keyboard, mouse and even the printer.

Unit 4: Computer hardware

Obviously the most important part of any hardware system is the computer itself, and the heart of any computer is the microprocessor which carries out the major functions of the system. The microprocessor 'chip' plays a crucial role in determining the power and speed of a computer. A microprocessor is basically a collection of switches that can be either on or off. Many millions of these switches can be placed on a single microprocessor, and it is these that give the modern computer its power.

4.2 Memory

Apart from the computer's ability to carry out instructions extremely quickly it also needs to be able to *store* instructions and data. To do this, the computer makes use of two types of storage – *external* storage (using devices such as floppy or hard disks) and *internal* memory which is part of the computer itself.

There are two different types of memory. The first is memory that holds information stored *permanently* within a chip and is only used by the computer to *read* information *from*. This is called Read Only Memory (known as ROM) since information is transferred in one direction – *into* the computer.

The other type of memory is called Random Access Memory (known as RAM) and allows data and instructions to be transferred *to* and *from* the computer. It is in RAM that the computer stores data that it is about to process, has just processed or may be needed for processing. RAM will only hold information whilst electricity is passing through it. When the machine is switched off and the current removed, whatever is held in RAM will be lost.

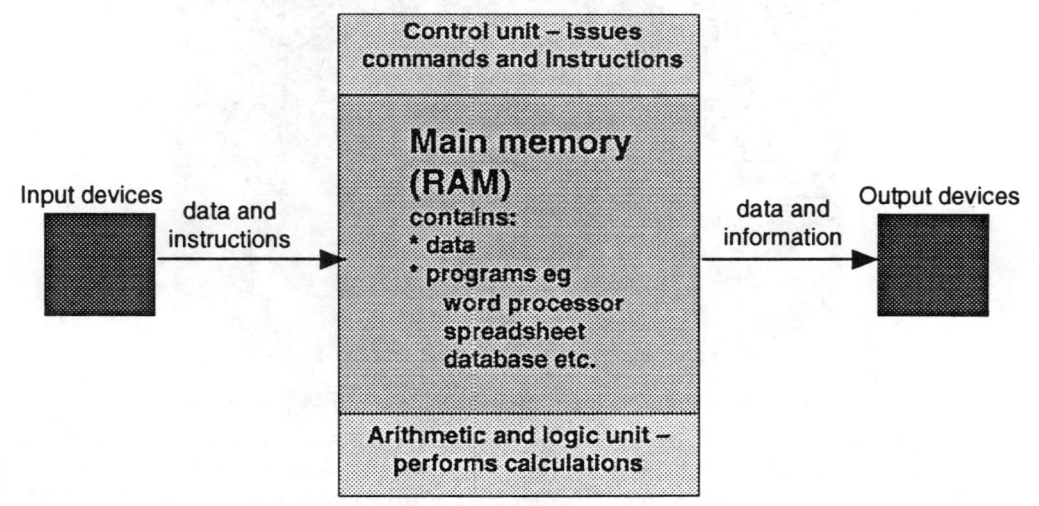

```
                    ┌──────────────────────────────┐
                    │ Control unit – issues        │
                    │ commands and instructions    │
                    ├──────────────────────────────┤
                    │                              │
                    │   Main memory                │
  Input devices     │   (RAM)                      │     Output devices
   ┌────────┐ data and │                              │ data and   ┌────────┐
   │        │──────────▶│   contains:                  │──────────▶│        │
   │        │ instructions │   * data                     │ information │        │
   └────────┘          │   * programs eg              │            └────────┘
                       │       word processor         │
                       │       spreadsheet            │
                       │       database etc.          │
                       ├──────────────────────────────┤
                       │ Arithmetic and logic unit –  │
                       │ performs calculations        │
                       └──────────────────────────────┘
```

The main memory in the central processing unit

The number of instructions and amount of data that a computer's memory can actually store is measured in *bytes*, as are other forms of storage. One byte holds eight *bits*. A bit is one digit (either 0 or 1). Normally eight digits will be required to 'describe' one letter or number. Therefore it is usual to think that one byte equals one character. The normal measurement of memory is either a *Kilobyte* or a *Megabyte*. A Kilobyte is 1,024 bytes and is often referred to as a Kb. A Megabyte is 1,048,576 bytes and is often referred to as a Mb.

Most personal computers sold today will have Random Access Memory capacities of at least 2Mb, often they will have 4Mb, but not usually more than 20Mb. Since microprocessors and application programs have become more powerful it has become essential to have larger memory capacity. Now even home computers have at least 1 Mb of RAM.

Section 2
4.3 Development
The fundamental features of a computer today are the same as when they were first developed around the 1940's. For a computer then and now to be useful it must have the following basic characteristics:

- ☐ some way of having data put in
- ☐ some way of storing the data
- ☐ some way of processing the data
- ☐ some way of being able to communicate the information

The overriding trend in computer development has been to increase the power of the computers enormously, while reducing the size. A major step in this development was the introduction of the microprocessor. This allowed for many different circuits, or switches, to be 'etched' onto a small chip of silicon. It was soon discovered that one chip of silicon could hold all the switches needed for the main processing unit of a computer. Thus, a computer processor can be fitted on a piece of silicon the size of a thumb nail.

An example of an early mainframe computer – IBM 360 Model 65

This development has had a huge effect. It has allowed the costs of computing to fall and has led to the growth in popularity of the personal computer. As demand has increased so mass production has allowed for prices to fall further, and as prices have fallen demand has increased once again. Thus a personal computer costing £700 today is about ten times as powerful as a computer costing £3000 ten years ago.

As computers developed they became divided into three main types. These divisions are mainly related to their size and use and are not rigid distinctions.

Mainframe computers have grown out of the earliest computers and are very large systems which allow large numbers of users access at one time. They are used by large companies and institutions.

Mini-computers are smaller computers which allow access by more than one user. They are used by medium sized companies and institutions.

Micro-computers are the smallest computers and were originally designed for use by one person at a time.

As the power of computers has developed however, these distinctions have begun to break down. Today many 'personal' micro-computers (or PCs) are linked together into networks and they have as much processing power as mini or even mainframe computers.

4.4 Types of Processor

At the heart of any computer system is the central processing unit which actually carries out the processing function of the computer. The speed at which a processor carries out instructions is measured in Megahertz (Mhz). So, if two microprocessors can carry out the same number of instructions, but one has a higher Mhz speed, it is the more powerful. The speed of the processor is determined by the type of chip it contains.

More powerful microprocessors are needed to handle the more complex programs. Any programs that make use of graphics, eg Windows programs or desktop publishing programs, and even many modern word processors, will require the more powerful microprocessors.

Microprocessor families

The development of microprocessors has resulted in a range of related chips increasing in power and speed.

IBM PC XT using the Intel 8086

☐ Intel chips

8086/8 This chip was the one first used in the very early 1980's in the first IBM personal computers. It is considered rather slow and under-powered today. It is sometimes called the XT chip after the IBM model it was used in.

8286 This chip was a further development of the previous one and worked at a faster speed and could make use of more memory than the 8086.

8386 This chip has the ability to process information in chunks of 32 bits at a time. The 8386 and 8386sx are currently the most popular chips for use in personal computers.

Section 2

IBM PS/2 model 55sx featuring a 20 Mhz Intel 80386sx microprocessor

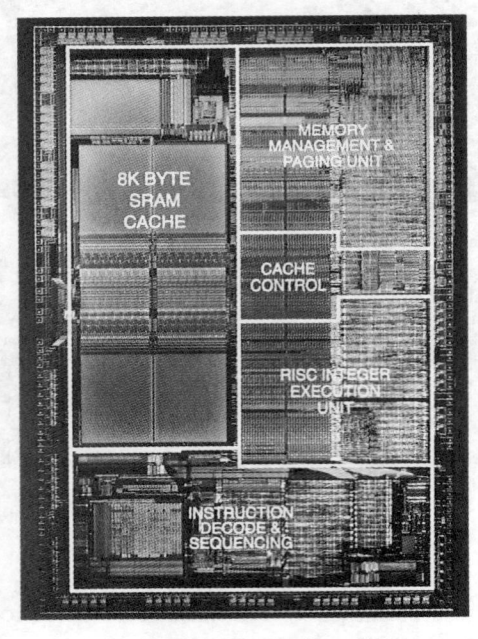

An Intel 8486 sx microchip

8486   This chip not only works faster than an 8386 chip and can carry out instructions faster, but it has a special *built-in* section that will deal *solely* with mathematical calculations. This means that for certain tasks it works at a much greater speed. The next chip in the Intel range may not be called an 8586 and is currently given the name *Pentium*.

60

Unit 4: Computer hardware

❏ **Motorola chips**

The Motorola company also produces a range of chips. They start with a *68000* chip, which was used in the most basic Apple Macintosh computers and in the Amiga 500 and 600 range. The next chip, the *68020* used in the Amiga 1200 and the Apple LC has not been widely adopted as it was quickly superseded by the *68030* chip as used in the Macintosh LCII and the Macintosh Classic II (or the Performa range). The latest chip, which is used in the highest powered Apple machines, such as the Quadra, and in the Commodore Amiga 4000, is the *68040*.

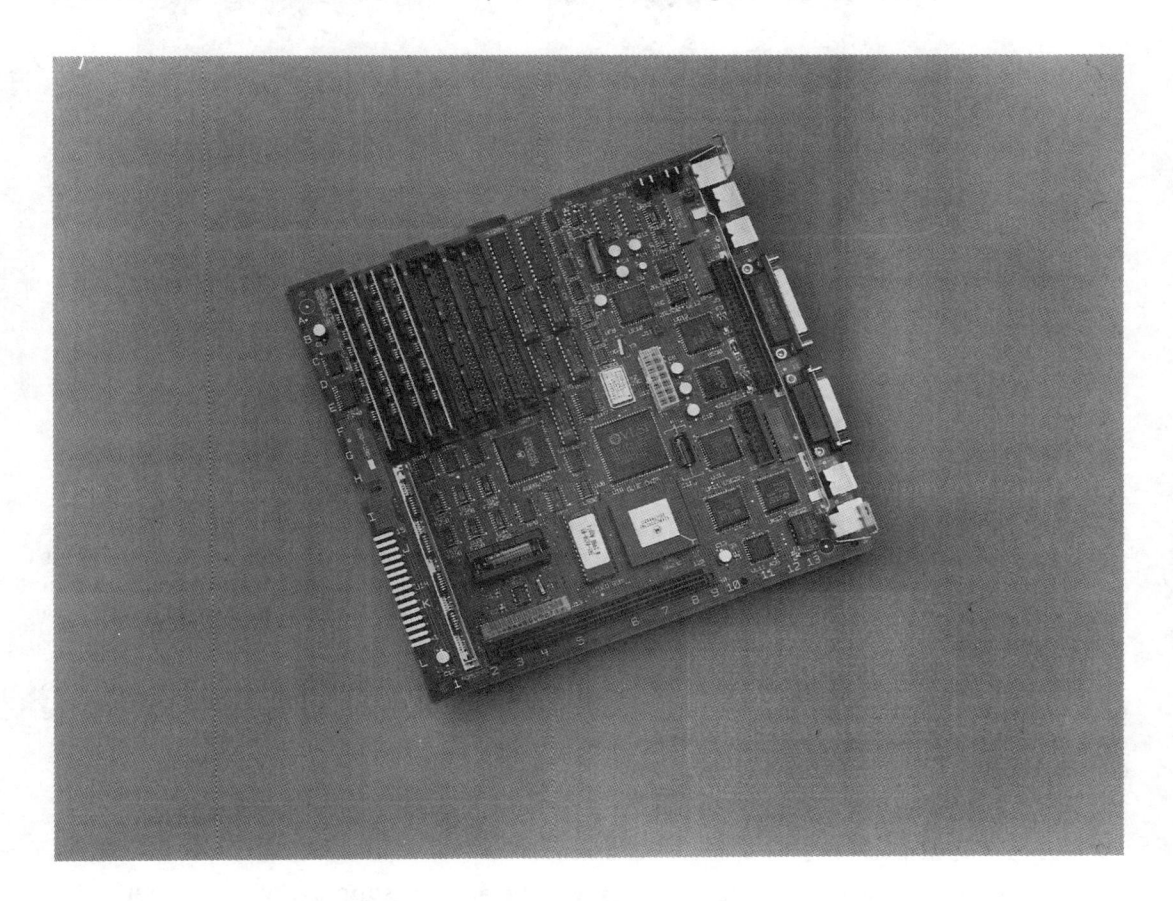

Macintosh circuit board with a 68030 chip

4.5 Display

One of the most used pieces of computer hardware is the monitor (or VDU – visual display unit). As its name implies it was originally seen as a way of monitoring what was occurring within the computer. Modern monitors have grown out of television technology. They normally use a tube and screen like a television. A monitor can be mono, which displays two shades (often black/white or green/white but sometimes amber/white), or it can be colour, which displays a number of different colours. Since the monitor is the major way that an operator receives information from, and checks information going into the computer it is vital that the monitor is clear and the information displayed on it is easy to interpret.

61

Section 2

Apple Macintosh Centris 650 high resolution monitor

There are a number of different ways of classifying monitors, the most frequent being the resolution. The picture on a monitor screen is made up of a number of small picture elements called *pixels*. The more of these that a monitor has, the better the 'picture'. Thus, a resolution of 640 x 480 pixels, giving a total of 307,200 pixels, is adequate, but not as good as a display giving a resolution of 800 x 600 pixels, a total of 480,000 pixels.

If a computer system is to be used constantly, or is going to be used with any form of graphics package, then a good quality display is essential. While all monitors must be compatible with the computer system used, a good display can make a system less tiring to use. There is, therefore, a continuing demand for better and better displays.

The development of IBM-compatible machine display requirements demonstrate this:

Types of display	Characteristics
Monochrome Display Adapter	This was the adapter supplied with the first IBM personal computers. It produced a reasonable definition but supported monochrome *text* only and did not allow for *any* graphics at all.
Colour Graphics Adapter	This adapter supported display in either two or four colours and could also display graphics. Its resolution was either 320 x 200 pixels or 620 x 200 pixels. Unfortunately this was at the expense of the quality of the definition of text, and operators often complained of eye strain. This adapter could be used on mono displays as well as colour.

Unit 4: Computer hardware

Enhanced Graphics Adapter — This allowed for up to 16 colours to be displayed and also had a higher resolution, (up to 640 × 200 pixels), than a CGA computer. It could also be used in mono displays to display shading. This display was quickly superseded.

Video Graphics Adapter — This adapter increased both the resolution and the number of colours displayed, (up to 256). The typical resolution is 640 × 480 pixels. It is now the most common personal computer display standard. Mono versions of this display are also available which display 64 shades.

Amstrad 8684

Super VGA — This is a development of the VGA standard which again increases resolution (from 800 × 600 pixels), and can allow hundreds of colours to be displayed. This standard may soon be the most popular.

Section 2

Unit 5 Spreadsheets

5.1 What is a spreadsheet?

In 1978 a Harvard Business School student, fed up with having to add up long columns of dreary numbers, came up with the idea of a spreadsheet. Over a decade later it has grown and developed into such a common business tool that it is considered essential in any modern business.

A spreadsheet program is an application program that can be used to perform a variety of business and mathematical calculations. It has a wide assortment of uses particularly for a modern organisation wishing to manage its income and expenditure more efficiently. It can be used to calculate production costs, depreciation on equipment, VAT and tax returns for the Inland Revenue, prepare profit and loss statements for company accounts, balance sheets and budgets for managerial support, analyse income and expenditure accounts, and create financial models for statistical analysis and forecasting.

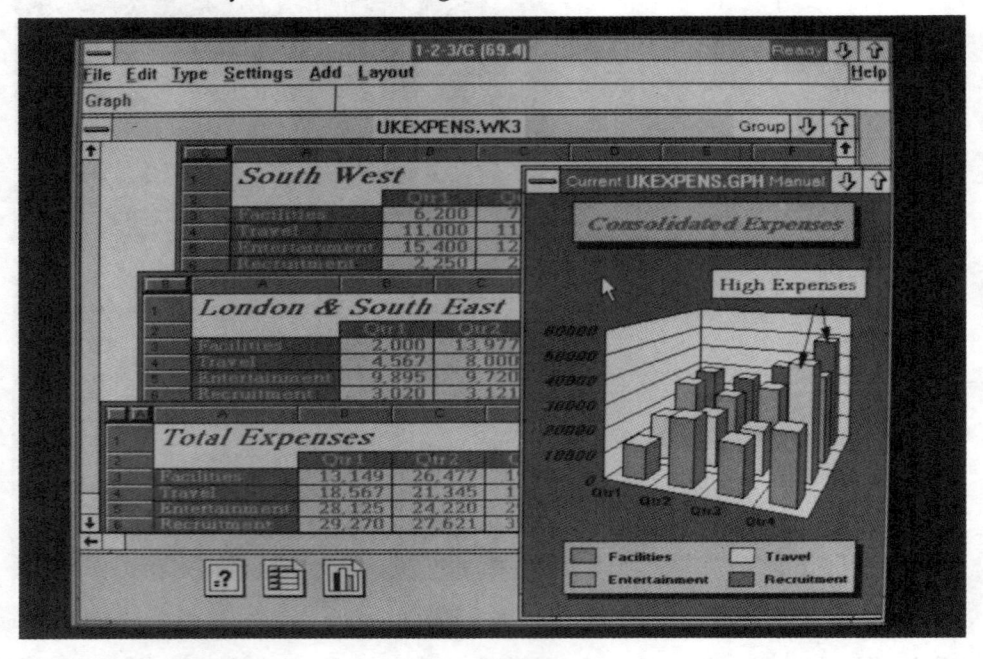

A spreadsheet package (here, Lotus1-2-3) can perform complex calculations quickly and display numerical information effectively in charts and graphs.

The spreadsheet program itself appears simply as a matrix of rows (usually numbered) and columns (usually alphabetical letters) that intersect to form a grid of individual cells, each having a unique cell reference or address. There are a variety of spreadsheet packages available and they all share similar characteristics. The more popular spreadsheets, like Microsoft Excel, Lotus 1-2-3, Mulitplan V4, and Supercalc 5, are very large and powerful, containing several hundred columns and several thousand rows and are too large to be displayed on a screen all at once. The screen, therefore, is used as a movable 'window' to move around the spreadsheet – a procedure known as 'scrolling'.

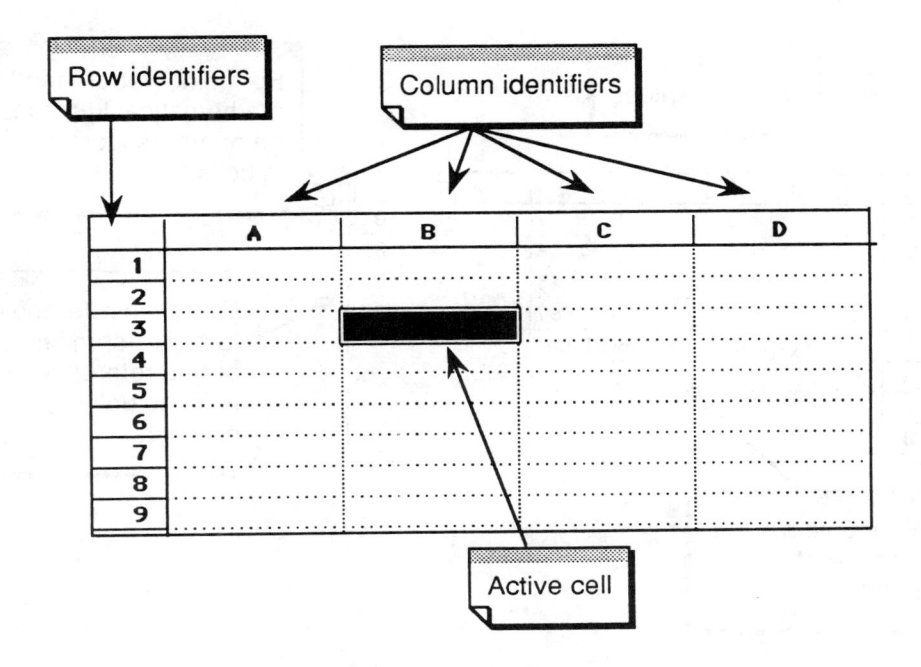

A basic spreadsheet layout

5.2 Data types

Data inputted into a spreadsheet is entered into one of the individual cells which is referenced by the column letter and row number – just like in the game 'battleships'. There are limits to the amount of data that can be entered into a single cell and this is dependent upon the program being used. All spreadsheets are designed to handle three data types: numeric values, alphabetic or text (label) data and formulae that perform mathematical calculations.

Data may be entered via a keyboard or imported or transferred into the spreadsheet from other programs. Once data has been inputted into a cell it may then be edited, manipulated, moved and deleted. The appearance of the data within a cell may be altered or adjusted and this is known as formatting the data. Examples of formatting data may include aligning text data to the left or right of a cell, and enhancing it by underlining or emboldening commands. Numeric values may be edited in order to display them as whole numbers, as decimal numbers or showing currency or percentage signs. The advanced formatting features of a spreadsheet vary according to the package in use.

Most spreadsheets allow data to be cut and pasted to other areas of the spreadsheet using simple mouse movement techniques. Columns and rows may be inserted or deleted, and more advanced spreadsheets allow the actual grids to be altered and changed.

5.3 Formulae

The flexibility of spreadsheets lies in the power of the formulae. The formulae perform mathematical functions and once entered into a cell remain hidden unless a specific request to view them is given. It is the *results* of the calculations that are seen in the cells.

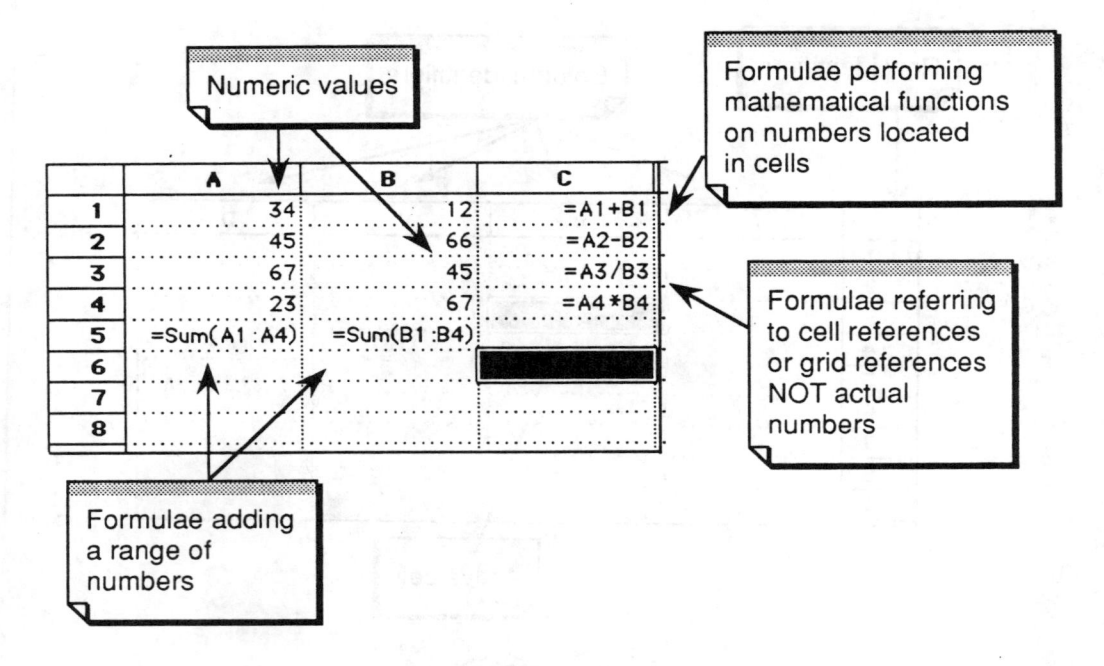

Section 2

	A	B	C
1	34	12	=A1+B1
2	45	66	=A2-B2
3	67	45	=A3/B3
4	23	67	=A4*B4
5	=Sum(A1:A4)	=Sum(B1:B4)	
6			
7			
8			

- Numeric values
- Formulae performing mathematical functions on numbers located in cells
- Formulae referring to cell references or grid references NOT actual numbers
- Formulae adding a range of numbers

Spreadsheet showing formulae

Formulae can be used to perform very simple calculations on constant numbers like 2 + 2; 12 * 5 (in spreadsheets * means 'multiplied by'); 8 – 3 or 144+12, but their real power lies in the fact that they can be instructed to perform calculations on the *contents of cells*. This may not seem particularly impressive until one realises that this ability means that numbers lying within a cell may at any time be altered and changed with the results of that change automatically recalculated every time.

Within every spreadsheet there is a bank of spreadsheet functions that can be drawn upon by a user. Such functions might, for example, total columns of numbers, find averages, square roots, etc. Spreadsheets, therefore, are powerful financial tools assisting in the decision-making processes of managers, but like any equipment they are vulnerable to errors. The accuracy of the results, and the decisions being made as a consequence of these results, are determined by the formulae themselves. Should these formulae be flawed or inaccurate then serious errors in output and decision making will occur. Because formulae are hidden (you only see the answer they generate) it is not always easy to identify an incorrect or flawed formula.

5.4 Modelling

The ability to change values within cells has promoted the technique of 'modelling' or 'what-if analysis' which has become an invaluable tool to modern organisations. Using modelling techniques an organisation can examine the effects of different decisions or propositions and determine the effect these would have on the organisation's finances. This allows them to experiment and explore with decisions and policies, analysing the effects of these decisions before actually putting them into practice.

For example, an organisation might want to know the effect on its profit if staff wages were to increase by 5%. Alternatively it might want to determine the effect that a 3p increase on the price of petrol by the Chancellor of the Exchequer would have on its transportation. Spreadsheet models can also be used for plotting predicted sales figures against predicted costs over a 6 month or 12 month period. This model would then be used to compare the organisation's predicted financial performance against the actual performance. Where there are dramatic differences an investigation into the cause of these can be made.

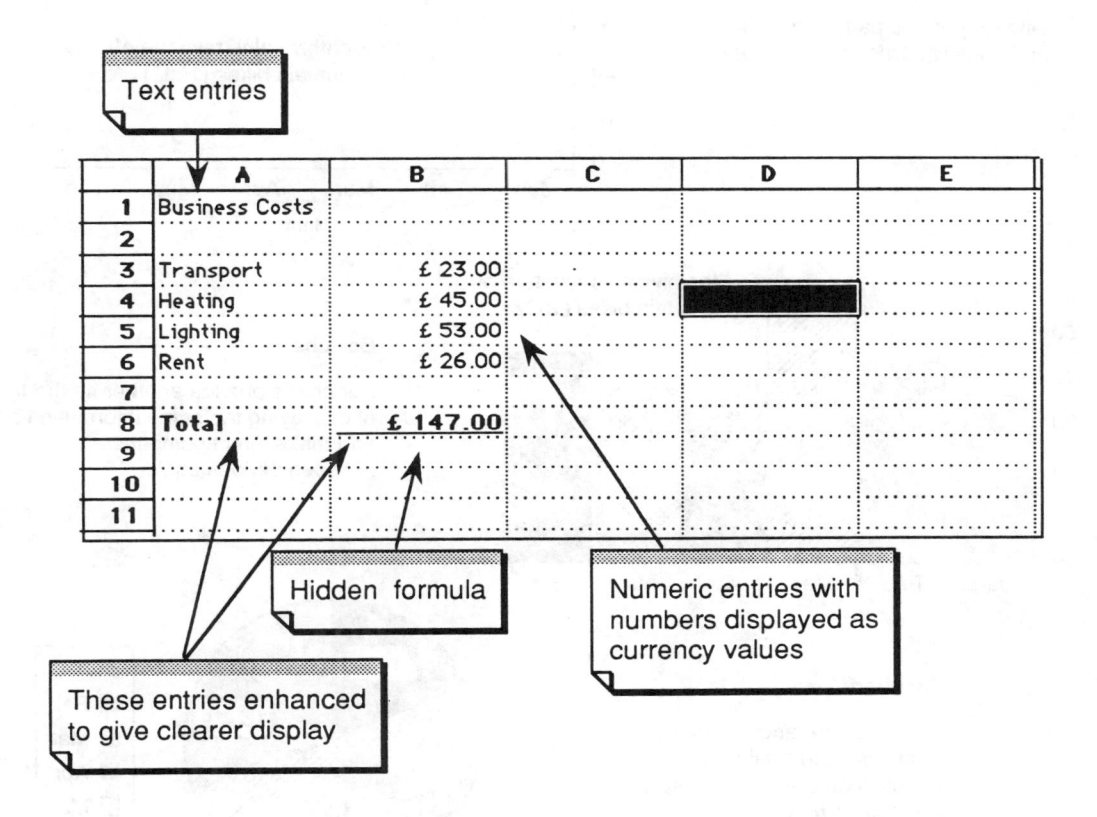

	A	B	C	D	E
1	Business Costs				
2					
3	Transport	£ 23.00			
4	Heating	£ 45.00		■	
5	Lighting	£ 53.00			
6	Rent	£ 26.00			
7					
8	Total	£ 147.00			
9					
10					
11					

Text entries

Hidden formula

Numeric entries with numbers displayed as currency values

These entries enhanced to give clearer display

A spreadsheet with text and numeric data

5.5 Charts and graphs

Most spreadsheet programs are able to produce simple graphs or charts from figures entered into the cells, providing a very useful tool for presenting colourless numbers as bar and pie charts (see page 68). Presenting numerical information in visual form often makes it much easier to understand quickly.

Section 2

Line graph

Line graphs are particularly useful for identifying trends over a period of time.

Monthly sales revenue of mountain bikes (1992)

Bar chart

Bar charts provide another method of displaying the same information, and make direct comparisons between periods easier.

Monthly sales revenue of mountain bikes (1992)

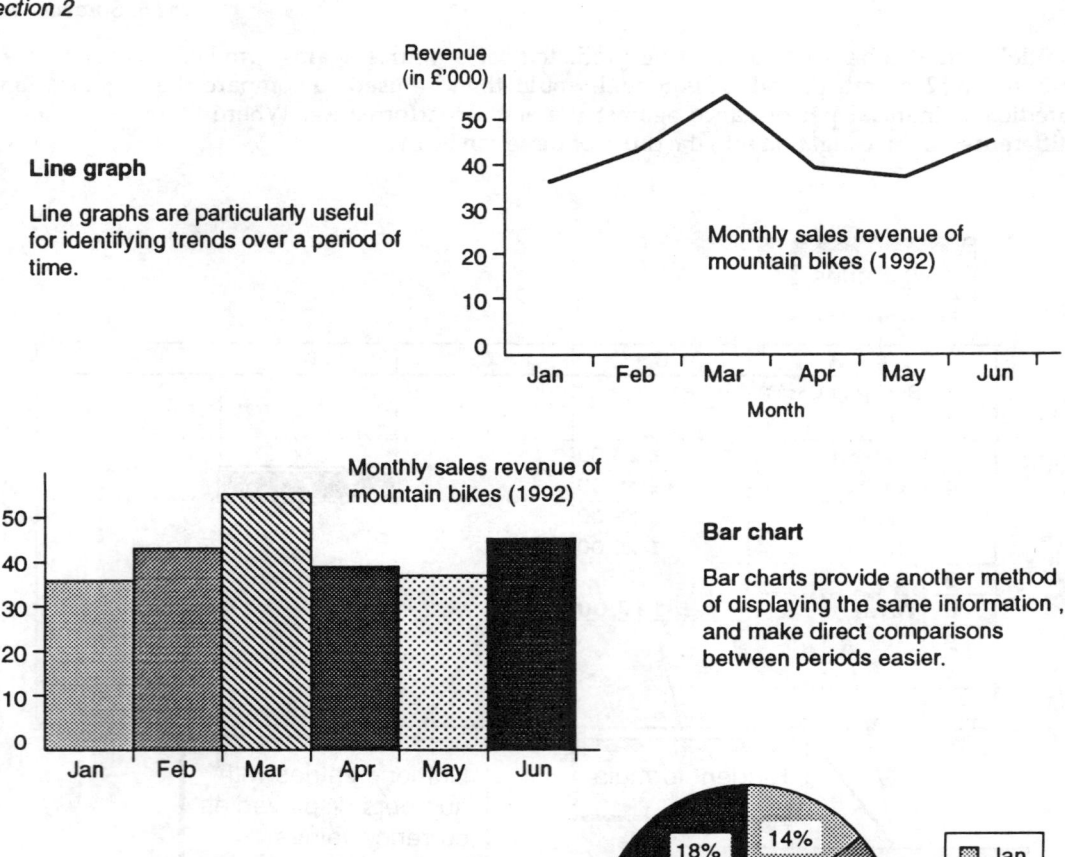

Pie chart

Pie charts are another way of displaying information. The calculations involved in preparing pie charts are automatically calculated by the spreadsheet.

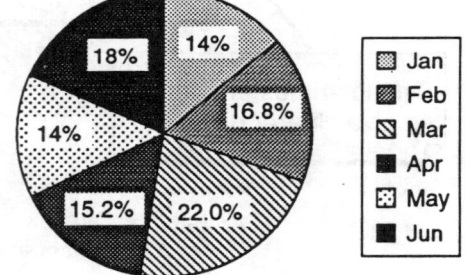

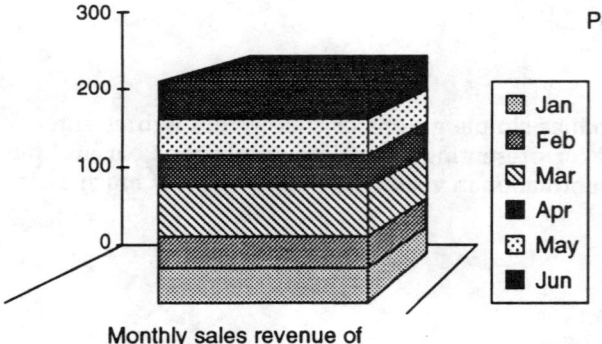

Percentage monthly sales revenue of mountain bikes (1992)

Stack chart

Stack charts, like pie charts, provide an overall view of the contributions made to the whole by each element. Three-dimensional charts are now becoming a common feature of spreadsheets and make the presentation of charts more interesting.

Monthly sales revenue of mountain bikes (1992)

5.6 Choosing a spreadsheet

There are a variety of popular spreadsheet packages available, and when considering buying a spreadsheet it is important to compare the relative merits and features of each one. As a guide, the features to compare are:

- size of the matrix, ie the number of columns and rows available
- the number and type of built-in functions available
- can Macros be written (short programs which instruct the spreadsheet to perform certain tasks, eg print a spreadsheet and save it to disk)
- the speed of calculations
- ease of use
- ability to import data from other programs
- the extent of its charting ability
- whether it is a two-dimensional or three-dimensional spreadsheet.

The most popular packages include Excel for Windows, Lotus 1-2-3, Planperfect, WingZ, Quattro Pro, Mulitplan and CA Supercalc.

Unit 6 System software

6.1 Introduction

Software can be broadly divided into two types.

- **Application software**

This is the software available for operators to use to perform specific tasks, such as word processors (processing text), databases (organising large amounts of data), spreadsheets (processing numerical data), etc.

- **Systems software**

This is a collection of programs that enables the computer to operate properly and to perform necessary functions such as accessing disk drives, monitors and printers.

For any computer to work it must be able to receive information, process information and output the results of the processing. To do this the computer will have to have some instructions to follow. It must have instructions on whether the information is going to be inputted from a keyboard, from a mouse or from a joystick. In the same way the computer will need instructions if it is to use a disk drive, a CD-Rom or a hard disk (see page 78).

These instructions, or programs, used by the computer to ensure that it is able to operate effectively are called the *systems software* or sometimes the *operating system*.

6.2 Compatibility

Different types of computer may, as well as having different internal workings, have different operating systems. It is not usually possible to use an operating system on a computer that it was not designed for.

Section 2

In 1981 the major computer manufacturer IBM was launching a new personal computer (PC). Their experience was in the area of large computers rather than in the personal computer market. They therefore approached a company which had experience of writing software for small computers. This company was called MicroSoft. They sold IBM their disk-based operating system which was called the MicroSoft Disk Operating System. It quickly became known simply as *MSDOS*.

The IBM personal computer sold well and many programs were written that could use the MSDOS. Other computer manufacturers realised that they too could buy this particular operating system to put in their computers and so avoid having to create their own. Provided they designed their computers correctly they would be able to use the programs written for the original IBM personal computer. Millions of copies of the MSDOS have since been sold to be used in computers manufactured by probably thousands of different companies.

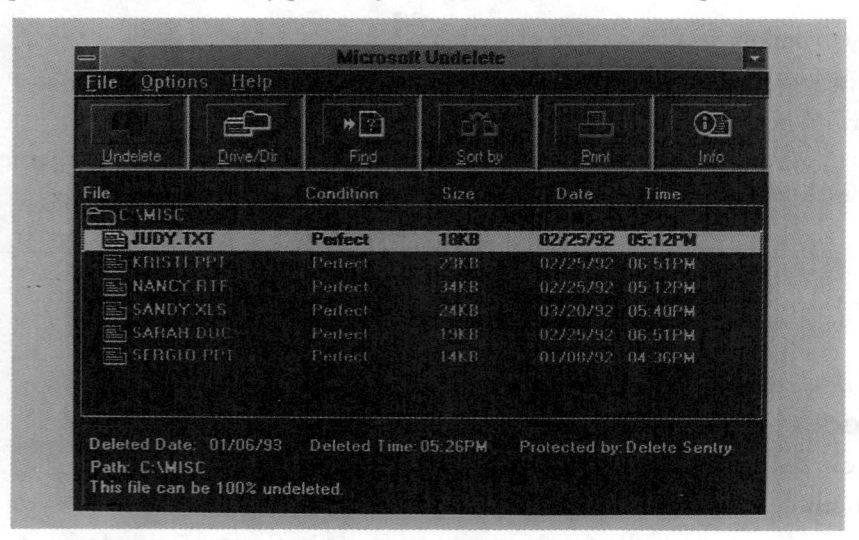

A screen from MSDOS 6

More importantly perhaps, it has meant that computers produced by different manufacturers can run the same programs, providing these programs are written to work with MSDOS. This is called being MSDOS, or even IBM, compatible. This has in turn led to a vast expansion in the number of these types of machines being used in industry. It has also meant that there is a huge choice of programs available.

6.3 Ease of Use

All PCs run on MSDOS and the only other system commonly available for this size of computer is the Apple Macintosh system running on Apple Macintosh hardware. One major difference between the MSDOS operating system and the Apple Macintosh operating system is the way they interact with the user. The original MSDOS system required the operator to type instructions or commands in a very precise way before it would carry out any operations, which is why it is known as 'command driven'. The user of an Apple Macintosh gives instructions to the computer using a pointing device (called a mouse), pictures on the screen that represent certain features (called icons) and pull-down menus with choices of tasks to perform. This method of using easily understood pictures is much easier to use as it doesn't involve learning keyboard commands and is called a *Graphical User Interface*, or *GUI* (pronounced Gooey). It has proved very popular and a similar system to run on PCs has been developed, also by Microsoft,

Unit 6: System software

called *Windows*. The Windows environment does not replace MSDOS as it is not an operating system itself, but is a layer between the user and the operating system which helps the user give instructions to the system. Most newer programs for PCs are now designed to be run under Windows.

The future for operating systems on personal computers is a move towards even greater ease of use. Whether compatibility amongst different computer manufacturers, which has occurred more by accident than design, will be retained is uncertain.

In large computers there are a large number of operating systems, but by far the most popular is *UNIX (UNICS)* which stands for UNiplexed Information and Computing Service.

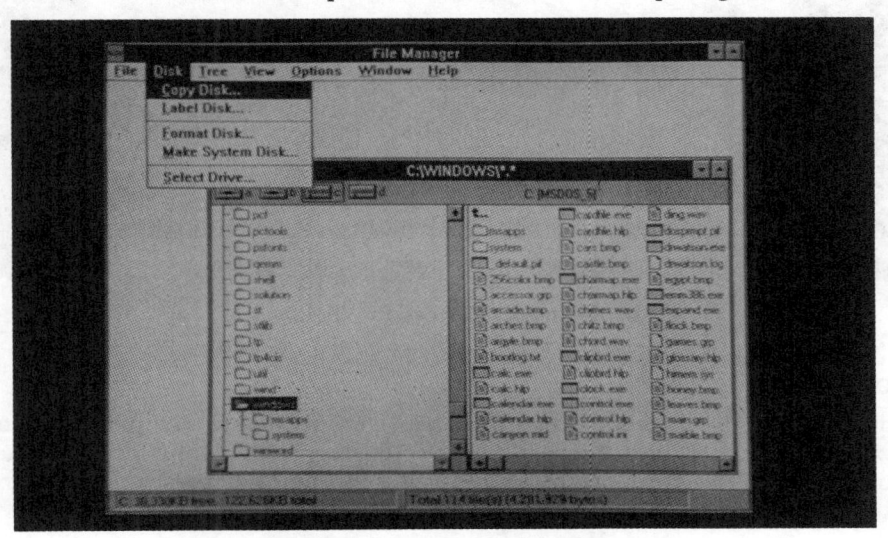

A screen from Microsoft Windows 3.1

Unit 7 Application software

7.1 Introduction

Software is another name for computer programs. The programs contain lists of instructions that the computer follows. It is important always to remember that a computer is simply following a list of instructions, and that it is never thinking for itself. All the thinking has been done by the programmers, when deciding what tasks they wish the computer to carry out.

Application software is the range of programs available to make a computer perform a specific task, eg to process text (a word processor application). Another type of software, system software, enables the computer itself to function properly (see Unit 6). There are many different types of application (including word processor, database, spreadsheet, accounts and graphics) and for each type of application there are different programs written by different companies.

Section 2

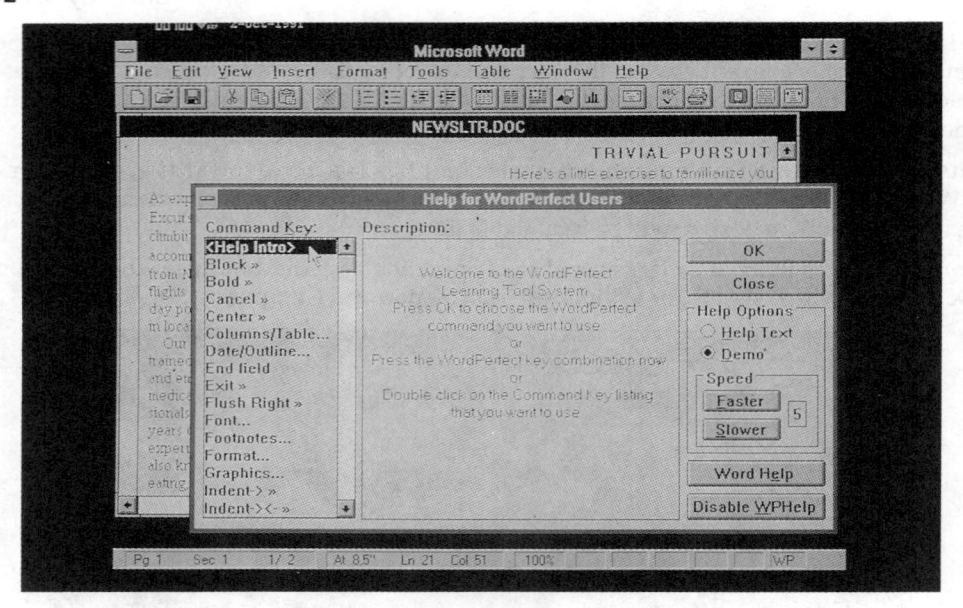

A screen from MS Word for Windows

7.2 Development

When computers were first introduced all programs were written for the particular computer they were to be used on. This customised or 'be-spoke' approach continued until there were enough computers in use to allow programs to be written and then sold to numbers of customers.

Whilst it is still possible to have programs specially written for a business, over 95% of all business programs in use are ones which have been written to be mass produced for a large market. The cost of be-spoke programs are out of the reach of many businesses, though some may pay consultants to 'customise' an 'off the shelf' package. So it is the 'off the shelf' programs that this section concentrates on.

7.3 Ease of Use

One important aspect of any application program is how easy it is to use. In fact much of the development of application programs has resulted from the attempt to make the different programs carry out more tasks and, at the same time, be easier to use.

There are, broadly speaking, two different ways to issue instructions to an application program. The first relies upon particular combinations of key presses, which the operator memorises, or has noted down. In the second the operator chooses the command required from an on-screen 'menu'. These menus will normally contain a number of related or alternative commands under one heading, for example if one wished to change the margins in a word processed document, the menu to be used might be the *format* menu. This menu might also contain the options to alter text alignment, set page breaks and perhaps tabulation settings. The advantage of a so-called *menu-driven* approach is that there is no need to memorise combinations of key presses, since it is possible to look through the menus to find the command required. Its main disadvantage is that it will take more time to make selections from menus than to use a *command-driven* system.

Unit 7: Application software

In fact, many application programs make use of both menus and commands, enabling users to choose the method they prefer. Where both approaches are available, the more experienced user will usually opt for the quicker command approach for frequently accessed instructions whilst using the menus for occasional commands.

Many applications programs allow the users to 'store' combinations of commands within the computer's memory that can be recalled by a single keypress. These command combinations are known as *macros*, and users can 'customise' their applications programs by devising their own macros.

7.4 Choosing applications software

Another factor which will influence which type of application is most suitable, is the actual hardware on which the program will run. You must check that the application can run on your particular computer. There is no point purchasing a program which makes much use of colour if the monitor you have is black and white. Therefore, when choosing applications software the following list is useful:

1. Does the package run on the computer I have or wish to purchase?
2. Does the package make use of equipment that I have or will have?
3. Is the package command- or menu-driven and which do I prefer?
4. Will the package be able to share information with other applications I have or plan to have?

Once these questions have been answered then the facilities offered by the individual application package can be considered.

Amstrad PC and Sega system

Section 2

Unit 8 Databases

8.1 What is a database?

A database is an organised collection of related files kept either manually or electronically.

While manual record-keeping systems store information and records on paper using ring binders, index card systems, wallet files and filing cabinets, electronic record-keeping systems store records and files on computer and computer backing store.

In a business organisation, large or small, both manual and computerised databases should be organised in such a way that they will provide logical and efficient access for their users. For example, data may be organised into personnel files, customer files, supplier files, stock files etc.

8.2 The basic elements of a database

Computerised record-keeping systems are built upon very logical structures and relationships. To understand these structures one must first begin with the smallest element.

❏ Fields

The smallest items of data that can be stored on a computer can either be an alphabetical character, eg 'a', 'b', 'c', or a numerical character, eg '1', '2', '3'. These are known as alphanumeric characters. These characters or data items are stored in areas called 'fields'. Fields storing alphabetical characters could, for example, store customer names and addresses or product makes and models. Fields storing numerical characters could store telephone numbers, dates of birth or prices of products. Each field is identified by its field name.

❏ Key fields

There will always be one field which is the key field and this contains data that is unique to a particular record and is used to identify a file. For example, on a hospital database there will be many patients sharing the same surname, so each one is given a unique number which makes the storing and retrieving of files much easier.

❏ Records

A record is a collection of the fields containing the alphanumeric characters. For example, the illustration below shows four records made up of six fields in which different types of data are stored.

Unit 8: Databases

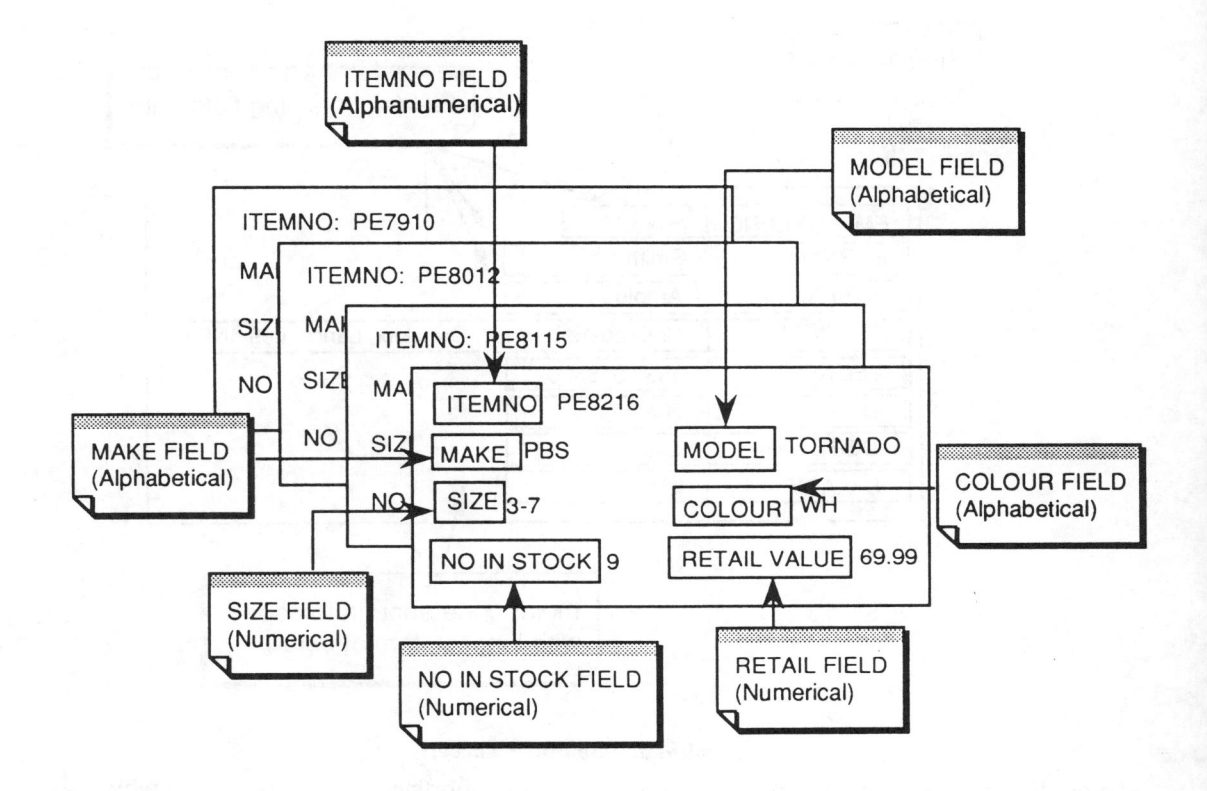

Records showing field names and types

8.3 Benefits of keeping records on computer

Once a database file has been created and data entered, it may be amended, deleted, sorted and interrogated.

Sorts can be made on any field and allow the user to organise data alphabetically or numerically so, for example, a database of names and addresses might be sorted by the Surname or Postcode field.

Searches can be made that will interrogate the data and select only those records that conform to certain selection criteria. For example, a personnel file may be searched for all employees who are over the age of 50. These selected records would be a subset of data that have a common characteristic.

It is possible to search on more than one criterion, so for example the list of employees over 50 could be searched for male employees over 50 only, but the number of criteria available to make selections is dependent upon the power of the program being used.

Section 2

```
Field names ──┐
              ▼
    ┌─────────────┬──────────────────────────────────────────┐
    │ EMPLOYEENO  │ AS2308                                   │
    ├─────────────┼──────────────────────────────────────────┤
    │ SURNAME     │ Smith                                    │
    ├─────────────┼──────────────────────────────────────────┤
    │ FORENAME    │ Arnold                                   │
    ├─────────────┼──────────────────────────────────────────┤
    │ ADDRESS     │ 12 Ledgate Terrace, Ormskirk, Lancs, L99 4NB │
    ├─────────────┼──────────────────────────────────────────┤
    │ TEL NO      │ 0569 645566                              │
    ├─────────────┼──────────────────────────────────────────┤
    │ DOB         │ 23/08/60                                 │
    ├─────────────┼──────────────────────────────────────────┤
    │ DEPT        │ Sales                                    │
    ├─────────────┼──────────────────────────────────────────┤
    │ SALARY      │ £15000                                   │
    └─────────────┴──────────────────────────────────────────┘
```

Fields containing field data

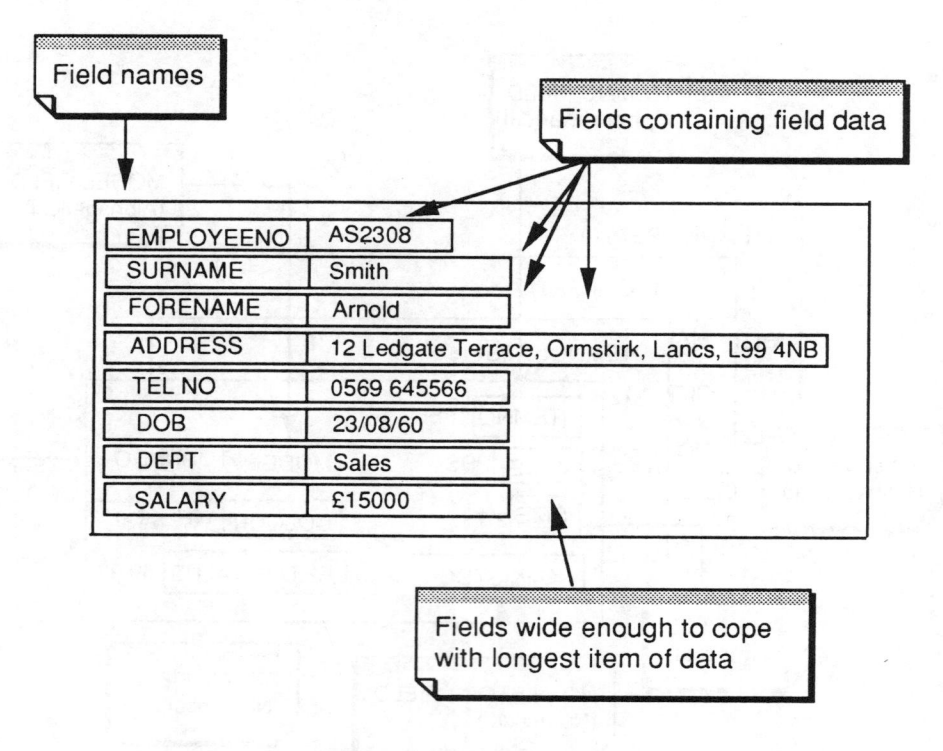

Fields wide enough to cope with longest item of data

Database 'Data Entry' screen

To produce printed copy of the data selected or sorted, reports need to be generated which will send the data to a printer. Printed reports are useful to managers for decision-making and analysis, particularly in the area of marketing and selling. A database of customers of a mailorder clothes retailer could, for example, be asked which customers have bought a particular item (or items) but have *not* bought another item associated with it (eg a jacket and matching dress). The database could print out the names and addresses of this selection on labels or letters, and the company could mail out some appropriate leaflet or order form to encourage sales. (The huge growth in 'junk mail' could be said to be one of the draw backs of the increasing use of sophisticated database programs.)

The ability to amend data, make insertions and deletions, arrange and sort files in different orders and make simple and complex interrogations of files gives a computerised record-keeping system a great advantage over its manual counterpart.

A manual filing system requires precious office space to store volumes of paper while a computerised system can store the same records and files on a floppy or hard disk. Even though hard copy is still required for lists of information, the quantity of paper is minimal compared to a manual system.

A Claris database, FileMaker Pro

8.4 1984 Data Protection Act

This Act was introduced to protect the rights of individuals by requiring certain obligations from data users when handling personal information.

The Act gives individuals (data subjects) certain rights to have access to information on them held on computer and, where appropriate, to have it corrected or deleted. This is known as the 'subject access right' and means that individuals are entitled to be supplied with a copy of the personal data held on them on request. Data subjects are entitled to seek compensation if damage has been caused by either the loss or unauthorised disclosure of their personal data. For instance, unauthorised disclosure of medical records might affect a person's success when applying for a job.

At the same time the Act also requires those who record and use the personal information on computer (data users) to comply with a set of Data Protection Principles of good practice, and register the fact that they are storing personal data with the Data Registrar. These principles recognise that data must be:

a) obtained lawfully

b) used only for lawful purposes

c) accurate and up-to-date

d) accessible to the individuals concerned who have the right to have the information corrected when incorrect

e) surrounded by proper security

f) restricted to information which is relevant to the purpose for which it is being held.

The Act, however, only covers data stored on computer and does not cover information held and processed manually, ie ordinary paper files. Neither does the act apply to data of a 'personal' nature, ie:

a) data concerning personal, family or household affairs

b) data used for calculating wages and pensions

c) data kept by clubs and charities.

Section 2

Unit 9 Hard disks and other backing storage media

9.1 Introduction

A hard disk, or Winchester disk, is an alternative method to floppy disks for storing data and application programs. The storage capacity of hard disks is much larger than that of floppy disks because data can be packed more tightly onto the disk. At one time a hard disk with 10 megabytes of memory was considered large, but today 80 megabytes is viewed as adequate. This is the equivalent of approximately 100 floppy disks.

The need for larger storage capacities has arisen because application programs like spreadsheets, databases, word processors, and graphics packages have become more sophisticated, and offer a considerable number of advanced features. These 'memory hungry' programs soon soak up available storage space, for example it is not unusual for a good desk top publishing program to require four megabytes of hard disk space. It is much more convenient to store this program on a hard disk and it is faster to run than if the program was stored on six or seven floppy disks. The success of hard disk technology lies in the fact that not only does it store and retrieve data very quickly and is capable of high storage capacities, but it is also relatively cheap to buy.

A hard disk consists of a sealed unit which may contain between one and five disks revolving at 3,600 revolutions per minute. The disks are made of aluminium and coated with a magnetisable material on which data can be recorded. Data transference occurs using a read/write head which moves back and forth over the disk, similar to the technique used with floppy disks, except that the read/write heads on a hard disk do not actually touch the spinning disk but hover delicately above the surface.

The read/write heads are very vulnerable to colliding into the disk if the unit is moved while in operation or if smoke or dust particles should infiltrate the sealed unit. Hard disks, therefore, need to be kept in a dust-free environment and heads need to be 'parked', ie landed on a special track on the disk before switching the machine off. Failure to do so could result in the read/write heads crashing into the surface of the disk causing irreparable damage to both disk and read/write heads.

Unlike floppy disks, the disks making up a hard disk are constantly spinning while the computer is switched on, and this continual rotation is the main reason why data can be read to and from the disk at a much greater speed than a floppy disk. Hard disks have storage capacities of anything up two gigabytes and this capacity grows each year as the technology becomes more refined.

9.2 Optical disks

Data can also be stored optically. At present the most popular form of optical disk storage is the CD-ROM (Compact Disk Read Only Memory) which look like the audio CDs purchased from high street shops. They are described as 'Read Only' because they have data written on them which cannot be removed. The disk is made up of a Tellurium alloy material which is sandwiched between two transparent layers of plastic that keep the dust and dirt from the recorded material.

They are mainly used for storing very large quantities of data, for example reference material like the complete works of Dickens or Shakespeare, dictionaries, geographical guides and encyclopaedias. These disks provide upwards of 650 Mb of storage capacity or the equivalent of 500 floppy disks and, like their audio counterparts, they are less prone to damage than magnetic

Unit 9: Hard disks and other backing storage media

disks because nothing actually touches the recording layer except a beam of light. They are also less prone to head crashes.

9.3 Magneto-optical disk

Magneto-optical disks are a development from the original CD-ROM technology described above. However, the main difference is that data can be erased after it has been written on to the optical disk, and new data rewritten to it. These disks have storage capacities of up to 128 Mb on a single 3.5" disk providing the user with a robust, high storage capacity. They are, however, very expensive to purchase.

9.4 Magnetic tape

Magnetic tapes are commonly used in large-scale computer installations where there are large amounts of data to be processed each day. They are used for storing large batches of data where fast access to files is not essential. They are a cheap means of storing massive amounts of data, but access is slow because data is stored sequentially. One roll of magnetic tape can store up to 100 Mb of data.

Optical disk storage capacity

Magnetic tapes are not practical for day-to-day routine operations because accessing the data is slow. They tend to be used as storage for backing up data on hard disks just in case the hard disks are damaged and the data is lost.

Section 2

Unit 10 Data security and safety

10.1 Introduction

Data security is often an afterthought for individuals and organisations who, having installed all their records on computer, discard their old filing cabinets and paper files. However, computerised records, while offering many administrative advantages, are vulnerable to far greater risks than manually kept records. Data kept on computer is commonly lost through the following:

a) the computer or storage equipment failing to work properly

b) a reduction or surge in the mains power supply

c) fire damage

d) the computer or storage equipment being attacked by a virus

e) operators accidentally erasing, or not remembering to save, files

f) theft of computer equipment

It can be devastating to a company to lose information on, say, its sales, customers, orders, or invoices, and many would quickly go bankrupt if they were unable to find out who owed them money or who had ordered a particular product. To safeguard against such data loss there are a number of controls that can be initiated. These fall into the categories of physical, software and administrative controls.

10.2 Physical controls

Physical controls include locking the computer room in which the computer or data files are located and, if the room is on the ground floor, ensuring that the windows are barred and the door made of steel. Alarm systems could be installed in all rooms to sound if the room is broken into, a fire breaks out or if the humidity or temperature changes significantly (due to a flood for instance). In a large organisation security staff could be employed to patrol and monitor access to rooms and buildings.

Access to computer rooms and data libraries should be restricted only to authorised staff issued with identity cards. In some cases access can be controlled by electronic doors and staff issued with personal identity numbers (PIN). Voice recognition systems are a more expensive but a more secure alternative to personal identity numbers.

10.3 Software controls

In the event of unauthorised staff overcoming the physical barriers, software controls can be employed to deny illegal access to data. The most popular method is the creation of passwords which determine which files an individual can access.

Passwords not only act as a barrier to unauthorised access, but can also be used to give different levels of access to authorised individuals. For example, a sales assistant in the sales department will be given a password that will provide access to customer and supplier records only, while a wages clerk will be given access to wages files.

'Hackers' are people who specialise in trying to break through these software controls. Passwords should therefore be chosen carefully and sensibly and should avoid obvious numbers

Unit 10: Data security and safety

like 999 or 12345 or the operator's name. Passwords should be kept secret and changed frequently.

Data is vulnerable to unauthorised access when it is transmitted along the public telephone network or via satellite systems. It is difficult to prevent illegal access to this data as it is transmitted across public lines but it can be encrypted or encoded so that it is meaningless to anyone without the appropriate decoding device and cipher. Alternatively privately leased lines may be rented from British Telecom or Mercury communications which are dedicated to the exclusive use of transmitting data by the organisations that lease them and are much more secure than using the public telephone system.

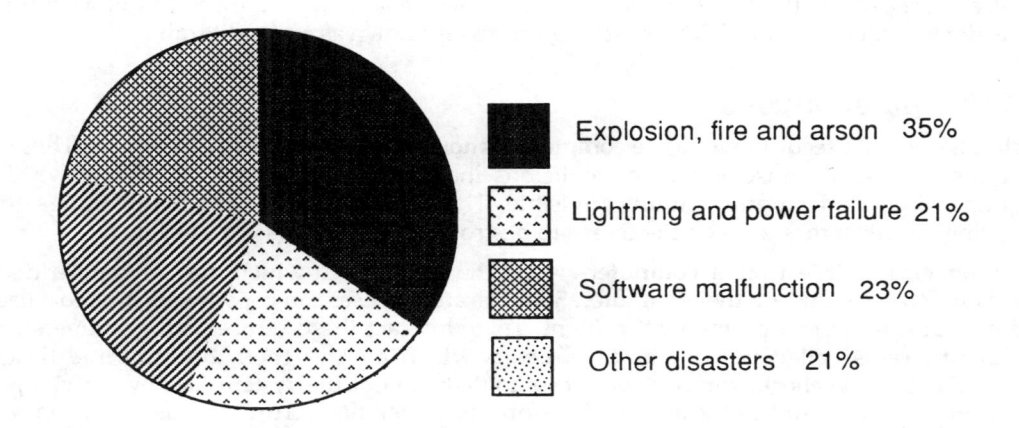

- Explosion, fire and arson 35%
- Lightning and power failure 21%
- Software malfunction 23%
- Other disasters 21%

Recorded cases of computer data loss disasters

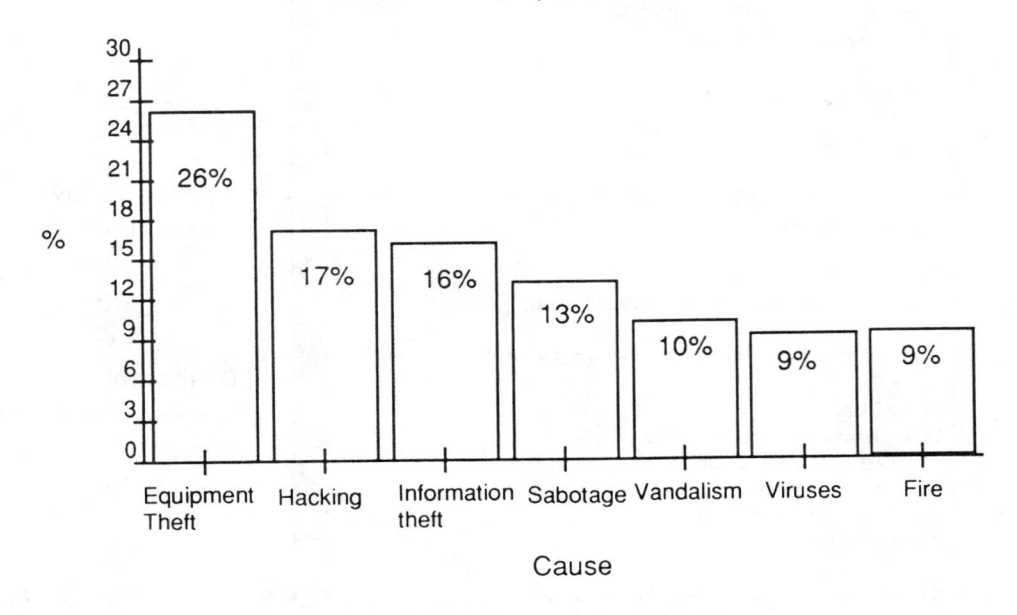

Equipment Theft 26%
Hacking 17%
Information theft 16%
Sabotage 13%
Vandalism 10%
Viruses 9%
Fire 9%

Cause

Computer crimes in the UK 1991

10.4 Administrative controls

More often than not, data is lost through the common human error of accidentally erasing files or through unpredictable system crashes. Whilst such events cannot always be prevented, measures may be taken to ensure that data can be restored. Such measures include backing up or copying the data files at regular intervals and storing these copies in a safe (fireproof) place. These backups must be kept in a different place from the master copies in case of fire or theft.

An organisation's data held on computer is open to abuse by its own members. To prevent these (and other) fraudulent activities all limited companies are required by law to have their accounts audited by professional accountants. Most computer systems today include programs which produce print outs of the day's transactions and these enable the auditors to follow through transactions to check for fraud. This checking process is known as an 'audit trail'.

10.5 Computer viruses

No chapter on data security would be complete without a mention of *computer viruses*. These are programs, written by mischievous or malicious individuals, which are embedded within a program's code and so are virtually invisible. These programs can do many things from displaying harmless messages on the screen to destroying the contents of a hard disk.

Computer viruses infect other computers when the program in which they are embedded is copied onto, or used by, another computer. Sophisticated viruses can copy themselves to a user's hard disk and become a permanent resident. To counteract these viruses, programmers have written programs called *vaccines* or *disinfectants* which are designed to detect and destroy viruses. The vaccine checks for unusual access to disk data or the system files by searching for known viruses. A simple precaution, therefore, is to regularly run a virus check on your computer and *always* run a check on floppy disks that have previously been used on another machine.

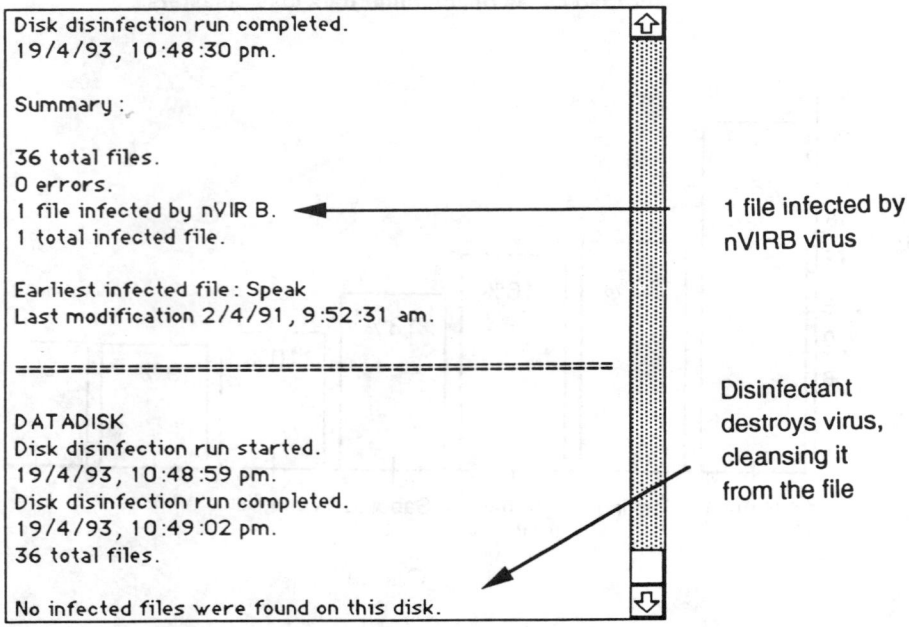

```
Disk disinfection run completed.
19/4/93, 10:48:30 pm.

Summary:

36 total files.
0 errors.
1 file infected by nVIR B.   ← 1 file infected by nVIRB virus
1 total infected file.

Earliest infected file: Speak
Last modification 2/4/91, 9:52:31 am.

=============================================

DATADISK
Disk disinfection run started.
19/4/93, 10:48:59 pm.         Disinfectant destroys virus,
Disk disinfection run completed.   cleansing it from the file
19/4/93, 10:49:02 pm.
36 total files.

No infected files were found on this disk.
```

Example of a report from a virus detecting disinfectant

10.6 Health and safety

The arrival of new technology within the workplace often promises great improvements in working methods and conditions. Out go the noisy and slow typewriter and old filing cabinets and in comes the bright new computer, complete with floppy disks and printer. New technology *can* improve conditions for staff enormously, but it is very important to be aware of the physical dangers of intensive use of this technology.

Computer technology is still in its infancy, and because most working environments have only introduced computers in the last 10 years there are few studies available which have addressed the long-term effects of working with computers. However, the research that has been done has highlighted many potential health risks.

Evidence suggests that computing staff who work for long periods at a time at monitors or VDUs (Visual Display Units) are likely to suffer from eye strain and headaches. In order to reduce these effects, operators should be given regular breaks of 10–15 minutes every couple of hours. In addition VDUs should be placed at a sufficient distance from the operator to reduce eye strain. Lighting should be arranged in order to diminish glare and reflections from the screen, and where this is not possible anti-glare screens could be fitted to each VDU.

Current EC directives recommend that all new VDUs be built with swivel and tilt adjustments so that their position can be altered to suit the individual needs of each operator. This will enable operators to adjust the screen to avoid light reflections. It also recommends that staff using VDUs all day be entitled to regular eye testing, organised and paid for by the employer.

In the United States RSI (repetitive strain injury) is fast becoming the most common occupational injury. It is found amongst clerical and computer staff who spend 6–7 hours a day word processing or entering data. RSI is caused when muscles groups, in this case the fingers and wrists, are used for intense rapid movement over long periods of time. Health experts advise that prevention is better than cure and suggest that operators be given regular breaks to rest their fingers and wrists, and have their jobs redesigned so that they also perform other clerical duties away from the VDUs.

Another serious concern is the level of radiation emitting from the screen. While there is not conclusive evidence to suggest there is any long-term damage caused through exposure to VDU screens, pregnant women are advised to avoid sitting in front of them in order to protect their unborn children, or to fit their screens with anti-radiation screens (often incorporated into an anti-glare screen).

Research has shown backache to be another major ailment in computer operators, caused by sitting in the same position for hours at a time. VDU staff should be supplied with adjustable chairs with height and tilt control, good back support and no arm rests. Noise pollution can also adversely effect staff, and noisy printers that are in operation all day should be fitted with acoustic hoods.

Finally, computer equipment should be located in well ventilated rooms. A room full of computers which are switched on all day will raise the temperature significantly.

Unit 11 Computer graphics

11.1 Types of graphics package

There are many types of graphics packages available offering a variety of features that enable you to draw and paint images, and then alter and edit them. The packages can be divided into two main types: draw packages and paint packages.

Draw packages create images from numerical information, ie they know that a line drawn on the screen is from one point at a particular coordinate to another point at another coordinate. You could say, therefore, that they 'think' of a line as joining two points, and that they 'see' the total image as made up of a combination of shapes or objects that can be precisely defined. This means for the user that the package can produce extremely accurate illustrations, ideal for, say, technical drawings, which can be adapted and altered. However, drawing programs can be very expensive and take up a lot of memory, and images can be slow to draw on screen. Draw programs include: Aldus Freehand, Adobe Illustrator, CorelDraw, Macdraw.

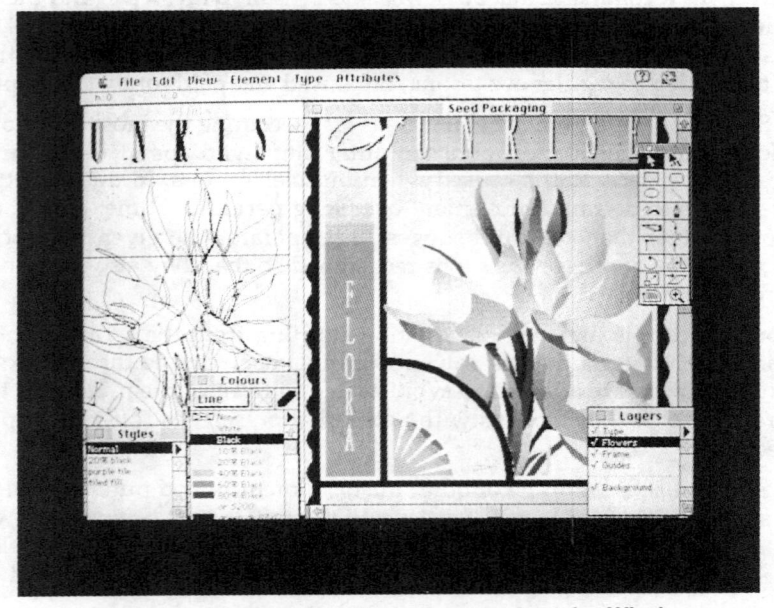

Creating an image using Aldus Freehand 3.1 for Windows

Paint packages create images by giving each pixel (the tiny boxes that make up the grid of the VDU screen or monitor) a particular shade of black or white (or colour if you are using a colour screen). If you imagine looking at the image with a magnifying glass, you would see that it is 'bitmapped', ie made up of tiny squares, and all the diagonal lines have jagged edges.

Paint packages are ideal for freehand sketches or for quick and easy-to-produce images that don't need to be precise. A disadvantage is that many paint programs do not allow an image to be altered once it has been created. The packages themselves tend to be cheaper than drawing packages and simpler for the amateur user. Paint programs include: MacPaint, PC and Paintbrush.

Unit 11: Computer graphics

The pixels of a paint package

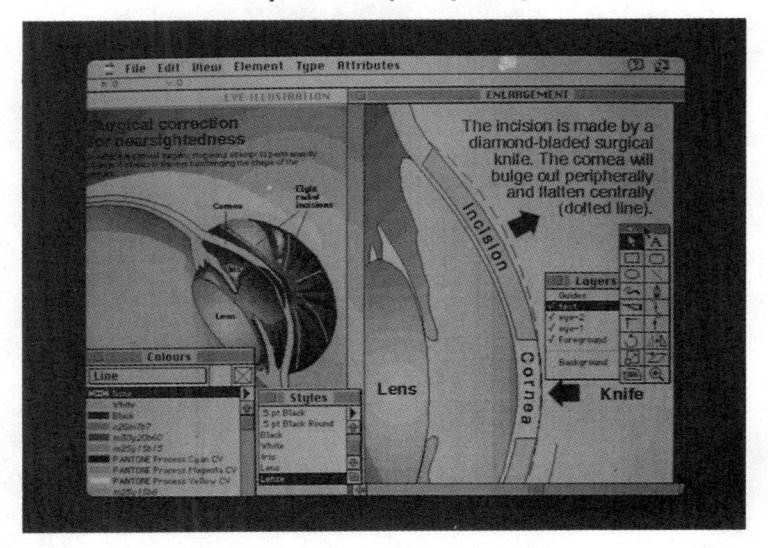

Making amendments to an illustration in Aldus Freehand 3.1 for Windows

Both draw and paint packages will usually be able to:

- create straight lines, cubes, squares, rectangles, polygons, circles, ellipses
- pan out and zoom in on a page
- select and move, rotate, flip over and resize an image
- provide a variety of patterned fills or colours

85

Section 2

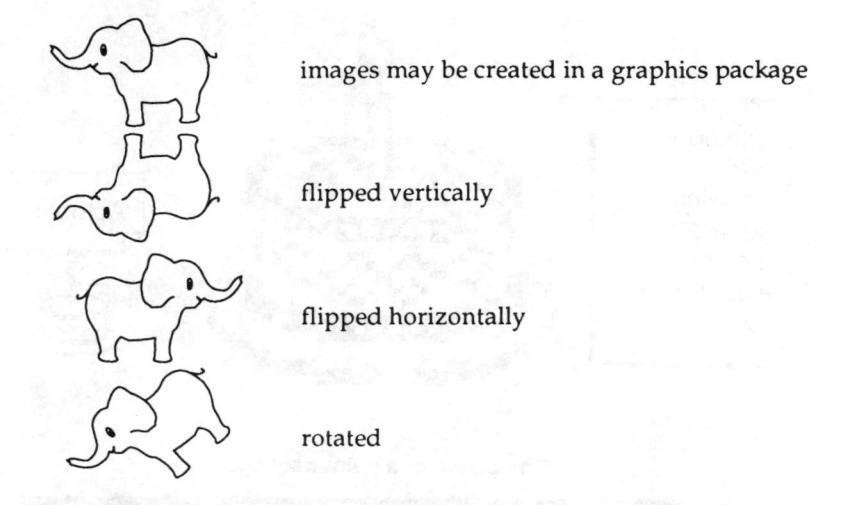

images may be created in a graphics package

flipped vertically

flipped horizontally

rotated

Typical paint tool box and effects

In addition to draw and paint programs there exist more specialised packages like photographic image retouching packages which can enhance and alter images, and animation packages which specialise in creating the illusion of movement on screen.

11.2 ClipArt

For anybody not talented artistically, drawing pictures and images can be a difficult task. ClipArt offers such users an alternative. ClipArt can be described as a collection of copyright-free pre-drawn images available either packaged up with a graphics package on purchase or bought separately. It is a software support tool designed to provide unskilled users with a large array of graphic images which can be included in a document.

Examples of ClipArt

Unit 12 Desktop publishing

12.1 Introduction

To produce a book, magazine, pamphlet or even a leaflet it is necessary to arrange the text in a fairly precise way (in columns for instance) and to include graphics as required. In the past this process was carried out in a number of stages: text would be prepared, illustrations produced and then the text and graphics would be arranged and pasted onto cardboard sheets together. From this final paste up, a metal plate would be produced and used to print the publication.

The process was very time consuming and not very flexible, since any change to an item within the paste up would usually involve changing the whole page and this in turn could involve changes to all the following pages.

Programs have now been developed that allow text to be arranged precisely and illustrations to be incorporated into the text so that the whole page layout can be seen, and amended on screen

Section 2

before printing out. National newspapers, for instance are now totally prepared on computer screen and the data transferred directly to the printing machine making possible many more last minute changes to the content and headline.

These programs have not only speeded up the process of page design and layout but have allowed for experimentation in design. Since all the changes can be made on a small desktop computer, these programs have become know as desktop publishing (DTP) programs.

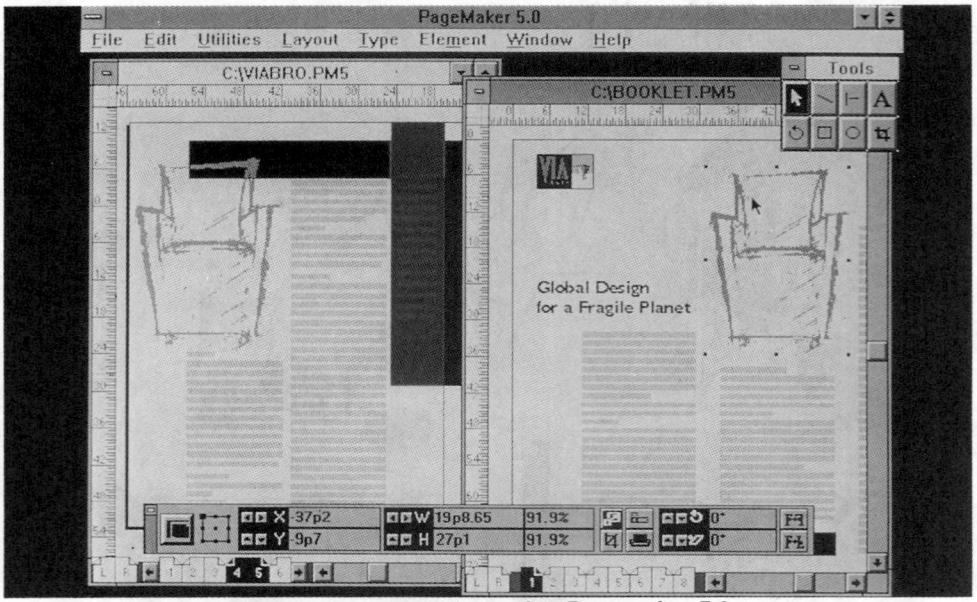

Putting a page together using Pagemaker 5.0

12.2 Types of DTP Program

Originally DTP programs were only available for larger computers, but as the processing power and memory capacities of personal computers grew, DTP programs became available for most personal computers. There are now many different programs available. They range from the very powerful, and expensive, professional programs which are used to prepare magazines and books, such as Quark Xpress, Ventura and Pagemaker, to the slightly less powerful, and cheaper, packages such as Timeworks, PagePlus or Personal Press, which can produce news sheets, promotional material and advertising flyers. They offer different features but all have the ability to combine text (often imported from a word processing program) and graphics (maybe created in a graphics package) on the same page.

12.3 DTP design approaches

Broadly speaking, DTP programs use two different approaches to the designing of pages.

a) *Frame-based DTP*

With a frame-based DTP program, such as Timeworks, the user designs a page by creating frames. These frames are used to contain *either* text *or* graphics and the frames limit the area that the text or graphic will cover. The frames that are placed on the page will not normally be seen when the page is printed out, although it is possible to make the frame print out as a visible border. Neither text nor graphics can be placed on the page without first creating a frame.

Unit 12: Desktop publishing

b) *Paste-board based DTP*

A paste-board based DTP program, such as Pagemaker, is very similar in design to the original paste up board used by traditional graphic designers. The user can place text or graphics anywhere on the page. There are no fixed frames. However, to assist with the page layout it is usual to have some form of guides which are shown on the page but are not printed out. The user can also create columns to contain text.

Major Features

Whilst individual DTP programs do differ, the majority will offer all, or most, of the following features:

- Columns or frames that can be linked so that imported text can 'flow' through as many columns or frames as it needs to. This saves considerable work, particularly with longer text imports, since all the text can be placed at one time.
- Text that can be displayed and printed in a variety of designs known as 'typefaces', and in a variety of sizes and styles (italic, bold etc.) known as different 'fonts'. This is very important for headings and captions.
- Detailed ruler guides, both vertical and horizontal, that allow for extremely accurate placing of text, graphics, columns or frames.
- The ability to display a wide variety of views of the page, from a less detailed complete page to a highly detailed view of a small portion of the page.
- The facility to set up a template that can be used as the basis for a number of documents or pages of the same document. A template would normally include the major heading (or Masthead), the number of columns of text and the margin settings for the page. Using templates saves time and ensures that all documents or pages follow the same format.
- The facility to *define* a number of text styles. A text style is a combination of the typeface, size and enhancement of the text.
- The ability to import and place graphics. Most programs have a number of features to allow the graphics to be manipulated. These can include the ability to re-size the graphics to make them smaller or larger, to 'crop' the graphics to only show part of them or to add to them using graphics tools.
- The ability to define how text and graphics influence each other. For example, you could specify that the text must run around the edge of a graphic at a distance of 1 cm or that a graphic (for instance a very faint image of the company logo) is superimposed over or under the text itself.

Section 2

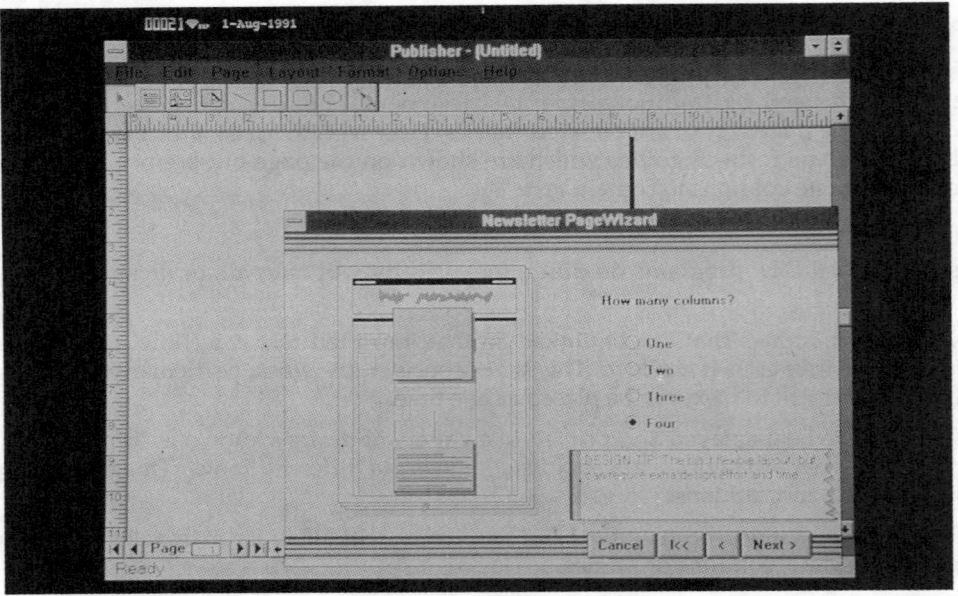

A recent DTP package from Microsoft, MS Publisher, is relatively inexpensive and aimed at the home user

Unit 13 Input devices

13.1 Bar code reader

A bar code consists of a combination of lines and gaps of varying widths that uniquely identify a product or commodity by holding information relating to the description of the product, its price and the supplier. To access this information requires a bar code reader.

Example of a bar code

Bar codes are used extensively in the retail trade, increasing the efficiency of shops and supermarkets, speeding up the input of price and product information by checkout operators, thus reducing checkout queues and providing itemised bills for the customers. If linked to a stock control system, bar code readers will automatically remove the items being sold from the stock records and provide management with immediate up-to date information of stock levels.

The bars themselves can be read either by a handheld light wand or passed over a laser scanner.

13.2 Mouse

An increasingly popular way of communicating with the computer is via a pointing device called a mouse. It is simply a ball held within a case that is designed to fit the hand. On the top of the casing are one or more buttons that enable the user to pass instructions to the computer. The ball has sensors that surround it and as the mouse is moved over, say, the surface of a desk, the movement of the ball is read and used to move a pointer on the screen in the same direction. Since this occurs very quickly it allows the operator to feel that they are moving the pointer directly.

The mouse was first launched by Apple Macintosh, but now forms part of most personal computer systems. It has greatest power when used in conjunction with programs that are menu-driven as opposed to command driven. It allows for speedy and accurate accessing of menus and also allows for easy highlighting of sections of documents.

13.3 Other input devices

☐ **Optical mark reader (OMR)**

Optical mark readers are devices which scan preprinted forms and use reflected light to detect marks made on the form. They have a variety of uses including recording answers in multiple-choice examinations, recording attendance and assisting in stock control.

☐ **Optical character reader (OCR)**

Optical character readers are devices which scan preprinted forms and documents for alphanumeric characters. These characters are intended to be read both by the human eye and the OCR, for instance those on gas and electricity bills.

☐ **Kimball tag reader**

Kimball tags are small punched cards attached to items in a shop which record the description of the item, the manufacturers batch number, supplier details etc. These tags are removed by the sales assistant on purchase and fed into a kimball tag card reader which reads the details coded on the card which immediately updates the computer. The computer will be linked to a stock system which monitors and updates the stock levels as items are being sold.

☐ **Magnetic ink character reader**

This device reads alphanumeric characters printed in magnetised ink. It is a system widely adopted by banks for processing cheques. One reader can sort more than 2000 cheques in a minute. Other applications include luncheon vouchers and postal orders.

☐ **A digitising graphics tablet**

This is a device which uses a 'puck' (tablet) to draw or copy diagrams and illustrations into a computer. A matrix of wires lies beneath the surface of the tablet identifying the position and movement of the puck and displaying a corresponding line or image on the VDU.

☐ **Light pen**

A light pen, which is a connected to a VDU, allows a user to draw directly onto the screen using a technology that detects the beam of light from the pen. The computer can detect the position of the pen and is used to display lines or point and choose symbols on the screen.

☐ **Scanners**

A scanner is a device which 'reads' artwork, photographs or text into the computer and stores them to be imported either into a graphics program, a DTP or wordprocessing program. It achieves this by 'scanning' the graphic or text into digitised form, as either a bitmapped image or a graphical object which can then be reassembled when required. (Object oriented graphics are

Section 2

better than bit-mapped images because they may be scaled up or down without distorting the image.)

Scanners can be either hand held, which are useful for scanning images from a variety of sources, including wall paper and brass rubbings; or flatbed scanners which require the user to place the document onto a flat glass bed to be scanned.

Scanners use different programs to read images and text. Images are taken in a digitised form, either as a bitmapped image, or as an object-orientated graphic, which can be reassembled when needed. Text is actually 'read' by an OCR (optical character reader) program that can recognise individual words rather than simply seeing words as an image of black and white shapes. As a result it 'guesses' what a word is likely to be if the type of a particular letter is rather faint. Some scanners can even read clear handwriting and other languages.

Unit 14 Output devices – printers

14.1 Dot matrix printers

Dot matrix printers are the cheapest of the various types of printer available. They are available in 9-pin or 24-pin versions. The numbers refer to the number of pins that are housed in the print head, and they are called dot matrix because the pins are arranged in a grid. The pins create an image by striking a ribbon which marks the paper.

Both 9-pin and 24-pin printers operate in two modes – a draft quality mode and a near letter quality (NLQ) mode. With draft quality the print head makes one pass to form the character or graphic to be printed, but with NLQ the print head goes back over the character or graphic again and prints more offset dots to form a solid character. Printing in NLQ mode is slower but the quality of output is better.

An impact printer from Amstrad

Dot matrix printers are suitable for printing sheets of continuous stationery, invoices, carbon copy duplicates and address labels. Their running costs are quite small, involving only the price of a replacement ribbon. They are known as impact printers because the pins physically hit the ribbon and paper and for this reason they are very noisy. The level of noise can be reduced by acoustic hoods which absorb the sound of the impacting pins.

There is now a type of dot matrix printer available which is capable of producing colour output. This is achieved by using ribbons containing different colours.

14.2 Inkjet printers

This is a non-impact printer (there is no contact between the print head and the paper) that forms an image by spraying ink from a matrix of tiny jets housed in the print head. As the print head moves across the page heat vaporises the ink, which is forced through the jets onto the page. Both the ink and the print head are integrated into a disposable cartridge.

A recent development in inkjet technology has been the bubblejet printer, which produces a better print quality due to the smaller and more numerous jets in the print head. The name bubblejet comes from the fact that ink is forced out of each jet nozzle by ink bubbles formed by heating the ink to high temperatures.

The advantage of using an inkjet printer is that the print quality is high and the blackness or density of the print is consistent. It also prints very quietly at a high speed.

The disadvantage of an inkjet is that it is more costly to run than a dot matrix printer and can't be used with carbon paper. In addition, because it is a wet process, large areas of black ink on a page might be smeared before it has time to dry.

There is now a type of inkjet printer available that is capable of printing in colour. Inside the print head are jets which can spray different colours, typically cyan, yellow, magenta (known as process colours by printers) and black. The inkjet printer has four reservoirs of ink, one for each of the colours. By combining these colours a wide variety of other colours can be created.

14.3 Laser printers

These are also non-impact printers, which create an image by using a beam of light to build up a pattern of positive charges on a drum. Plastic powder called 'toner' is attracted to the charged areas on the drum and then transferred and fused to paper that is passed over it.

Section 2

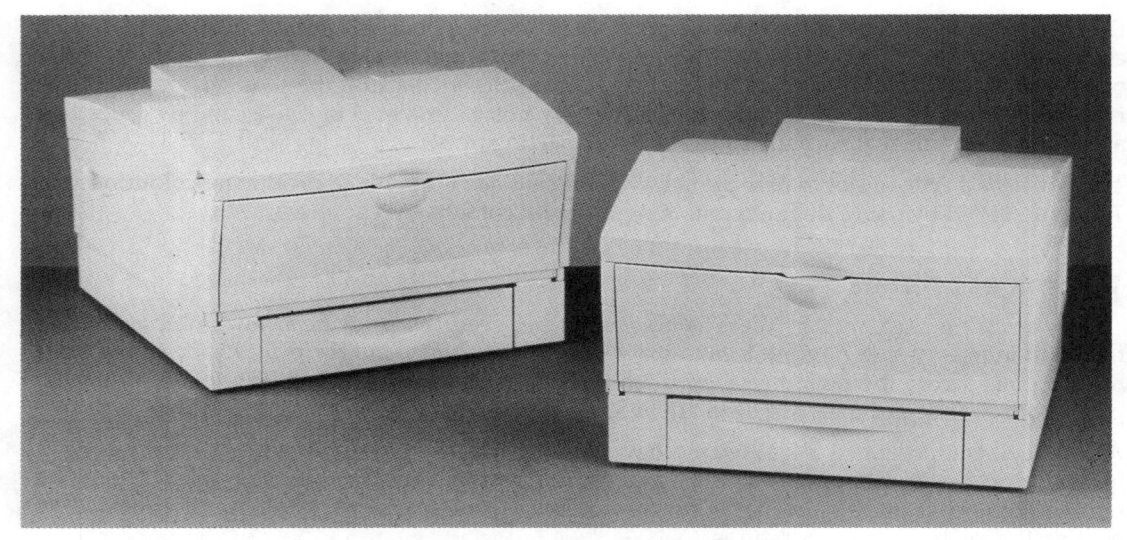

Apple LaserWriter Select 300 and 310

The quality of output is outstanding and they are suitable for producing professional-looking documents where presentation and display are important. Most laser printers output at either 300 dots per inch or 600 dots per inch, giving the characters they produce on the page a very smooth and sharp finish. They are particularly suited for outputting desktop published documents. The laser printer cannot produce multiple copies using carbon paper.

Laser printers are also capable of printing in colour. This is achieved by storing four colours of toner within the printer (cyan, yellow, magenta and black). To achieve colour output the laser printer will make four passes over the paper, one for each colour, enriching the tone and intensity of colours in the image each time. It may seem that having four toner cartridges to support printed output is expensive to run, but the toner from each cartridge is only used for 25% of the time (a black toner cartridge in a black and white printer is used 100% of the time).

Unit 15 Communication technology

15.1 Introduction

In today's 'global village' distances between countries and continents seem to be shrinking, due largely to the development of modern communication systems. There are few aspects of our lives untouched by the 'communications revolution'. At home pictures of war torn countries and starving children are transmitted across the world, bounced off satellites into our television sets. At work, up-to-date information can be accessed instantly from electronic databases located anywhere in the world and conversations between people thousands of miles apart take place effortlessly. Data of all varieties – audio, textual, numerical and video – can now be transmitted globally using a variety of telecommunication devices.

15.2 Public telephone network (PTN)

The public telephone network is one of the oldest methods of telecommunication, delivering voice messages into homes and businesses from people thousands of miles apart. At present there are over 700 million global subscribers to telephone networks and messages are transmitted using a variety of communication media ranging from optic fibres to microwave transmitters, undersea cables and satellites.

The main telephone lines are made of copper wire, but this cabling is gradually being replaced with optic fibres. These are fine strands of glass-like material which carry signals at the speed of light (300,000 km per second) and are less prone to message distortion. Optic fibres are ideal for handling digital information suitable for input to a computer or telephone system.

Subscribers to the public telephone network are offered a large array of advanced features and services on their telephone handsets, including devices which contain a microprocessor and internal memory for storing telephone numbers, and have last number re-dial, automatic re-dial, secrecy buttons, and LCD digital display features. Answering machines provide users with the opportunity to record messages from callers when they are not available to answer the calls themselves.

15.3 Cellular telephones

One of the most recent developments has been the emergence of cellular telephone technology. These are mobile computer controlled telephones – usually installed in cars – allowing users to transmit and receive telephone calls while on the move and away from a telephone socket. They are particularly useful for people who are away from their home or workplace but need to keep in constant contact, eg salespeople or doctors. Cellular telephones allow users to both receive and transmit messages. Simpler alternative devices like pagers exist which receive a signal indicating that the holder should find a telephone and call his or her place of work. Alternatively other portable devices like the 'Rabbit' telephones are only able to receive calls while in close proximity to 'Rabbit' transmitters.

15.4 Electronic mail

Electronic mail is a major development in modern communication technology. In general terms it refers to all methods of communication that electronically transmit letters numbers and images across the telephone network system, and include telex and teletex messages and facsimiles. To most people, however, electronic mail is associated more specifically with 'computerised messaging'.

In 1981 British Telecom introduced Telecom Gold (now called the BT Mailbox service), an electronic mailing service for subscribers possessing a computer which is linked into the telephone network system. This mailing service allows subscribers to send and receive 'computerised messages' to one another across the public telephone network system. Each subscriber is provided with a unique mailbox number in which messages can be left and read at leisure. Subscribers can exchange textual messages nationally and internationally with anyone connected to this messaging service. This method of communication, like other forms of electronic mail, has the advantage over the postal service of being reliable and fast. Messages can be sent at any time of the day from anywhere in the world and subscribers to the network can automatically collect, send and store messages.

Section 2

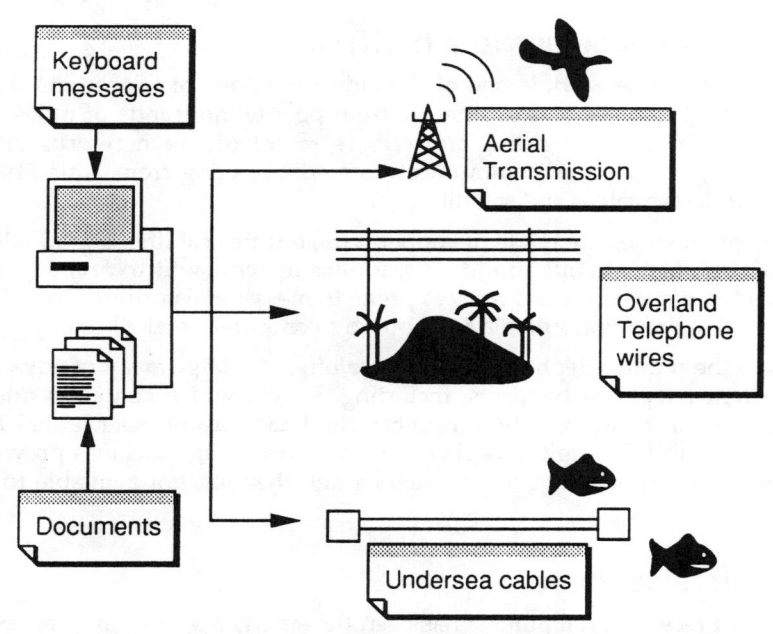

Three methods of transmitting Email messages

Because messages are sent across the public telephones lines a device called a modem (modulator/demodulator) is needed. This device converts or modulates the digital signals of the computer into electrical wave forms which are transmitted across the telephone wires. A receiving modem is needed at the other end to convert or demodulate the signal back into digital form again.

❏ **Facsimile (FAX)**

A facsimile machine is a device which is able to transmit and receive printed text and images across the public telephone system, 24 hours a day from anywhere in the world. This device is very accessible for most businesses because it is very easy to operate and is cheap to buy. It is much faster and more reliable than the normal postal service and can transmit and receive picture and photo images.

❏ **Telex**

Telex is over 30 years old and one of the earliest forms of electronic mail able to send and receive textual information. In the past, teletypewriters were used for sending and receiving messages, but these are being replaced with VDUs which allow users to prepare messages accurately and carefully before transmission takes place. The British Telecom telex system is linked to the worldwide international telecommunications network.

❏ **Tele and video conferencing**

Teleconferencing is a British Telecom service that allows more than two people to be linked together on the same line enabling a telephone conference to take place. All those involved in the conference will be able to hear each speaker and be able to make a contribution themselves.

Video conferencing is similar to teleconferencing but transmits sound and vision, allowing business people far apart to hold meetings and have conversations without having to travel outside their region. At present there are nine British Telecom public studios in England and Scotland which can be hired by the hour. These studios can be linked to any of the 450 public studios which are found in 140 countries around the world.

15.5 On-line databases

On-line databases are electronic libraries that store large amounts of information for access by a subscriber using a computer terminal linked to the telephone network. The actual location of the database is unimportant since users can gain access to it from any part of the globe.

There are a variety of on-line databases which store different types of data. For example, there are educational databases like Campus 2000 which allows schools and colleges and other educational institutions to communicate with one another and to access libraries of information relating to curriculum areas and courses on offer throughout the UK. Datastream offers businesses access to immediate information relating to the stock market, movement of shares and exchange rates, business takeovers and corporate accounts. Eurotex is a European database which provides users with access to a variety of information about European business law, international and UK law.

One of the largest on-line systems in this country is Compuserve, with over 700 members who are able to access news and current affairs reports, read consumer reports like *Which* magazine, and access a variety of on-line software support. In addition, Compuserve allows its subscribers to send and receive electronic messages directly through bulletin boards. Bulletin boards are electronic notice boards that display messages, advertisements and chat facilities. Because the data on the database is stored digitally, a modem is necessary in order to access and receive data that has been sent across the telephone line.

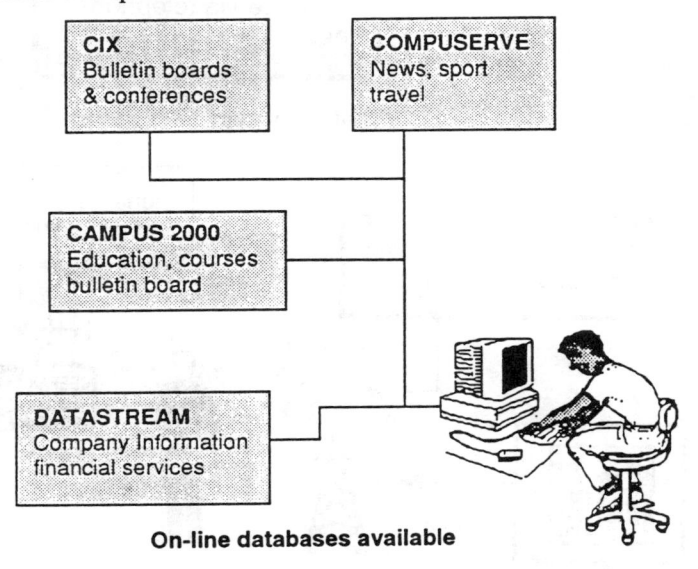

On-line databases available

15.6 Videotext

Videotext is a general term used to describe viewdata and teletext systems. Both systems store information on a central computer which can be accessed and transmitted to receiving terminals.

A **viewdata** system is a computer-based information system which accesses information stored on a central computer through the public telephone network and requires a keyboard, modem and telephone line to transmit and receive messages.

Teletext, on the other hand, is a computer-based information system broadcast as part of the television channel signal, and users can only receive and not transmit messages. Users have to pay an additional fee when buying a television, and the service can be found on all four television channels.

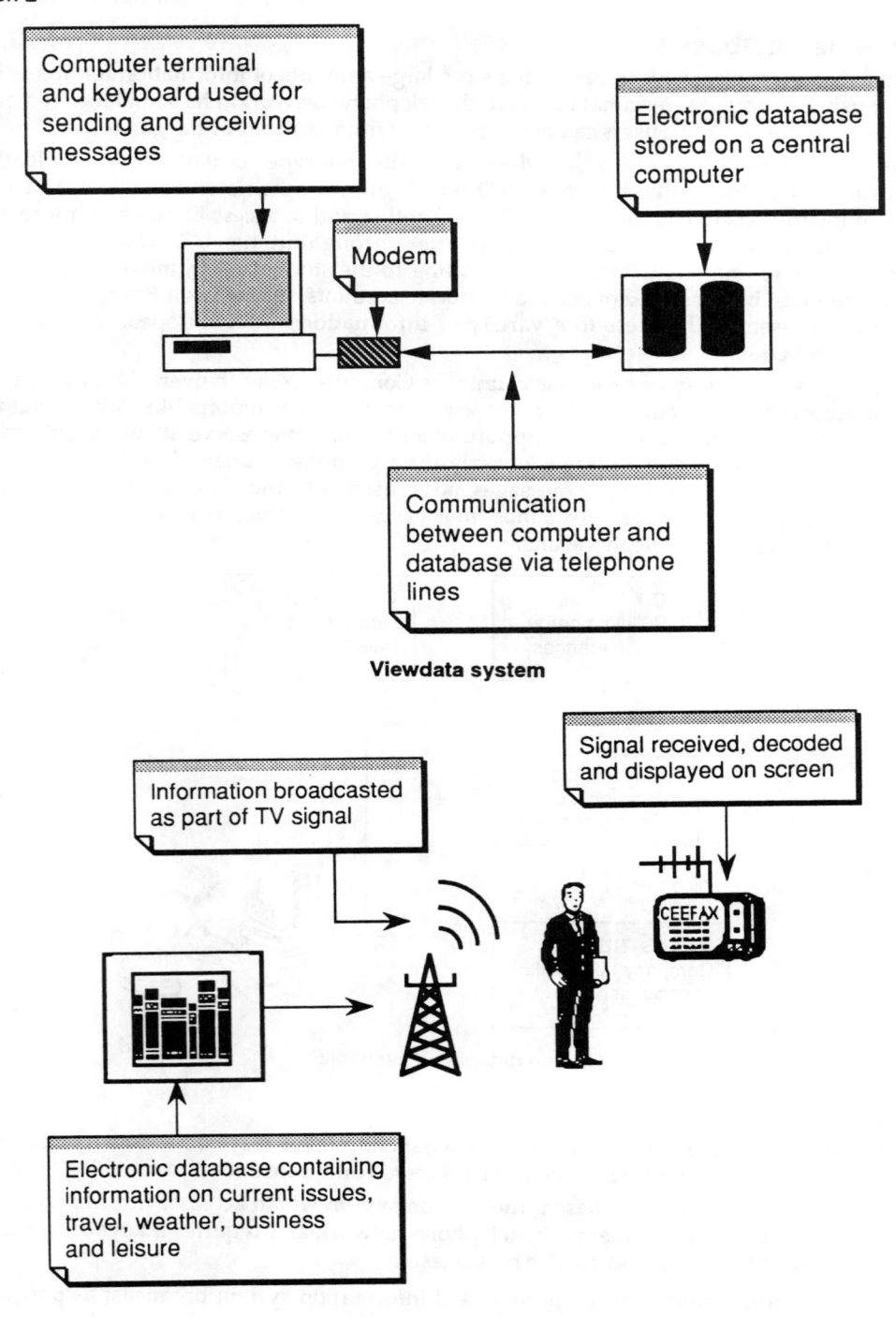

Section 2

Computer terminal and keyboard used for sending and receiving messages

Modem

Electronic database stored on a central computer

Communication between computer and database via telephone lines

Viewdata system

Information broadcasted as part of TV signal

Signal received, decoded and displayed on screen

Electronic database containing information on current issues, travel, weather, business and leisure

Teletext system

Unit 16 Accounting/Bookkeeping packages

Modern accounting packages have revolutionised two principal areas in business – the recording of daily and routine financial transactions, and the analysis of financial data into information on which to base important business decisions.

Limited companies are legally required to keep detailed records of financial transactions, which are checked periodically by auditors. Before computerisation, even a medium-sized business needed a large number of accounts clerks or bookkeepers to record manually the numerous daily transactions and create the necessary paperwork such as invoices, credit notes, statements, etc to keep the business running properly. Now, accounting application packages can perform these tasks quickly and accurately, and can do some jobs (such as creating statements for overdue accounts) automatically. Some accounting packages can also calculate all the weekly or monthly staff wages, taking into account tax deductions, national insurance and overtime, and print out the payslips.

Managers are able to find out quickly and accurately the information they need, such as daily sales figures, amounts of money owed to or by the company, monthly profit levels etc, for decision-making purposes.

Simple packages are ideal for small businesses to keep their daily purchase and sales accounts on. More sophisticated accounting packages can integrate many of these functions so that information from one area, say sales invoicing, automatically updates the latest profit figures in another part of the system. Some can also produce all the information the company needs at the end of the financial year, such as profit and loss figures and balance sheets.

These packages are only tools, however, and to use the more advanced packages properly requires considerable accounting knowledge and skills. In the same way as a DTP program can only produce documents that look as good as the design skills of the user, so an accounting program will only be accurate and effective if the user understands the accounting principles it is following.

Unit 17 Integrated software

17.1 Introduction

As the popularity of certain business software grew it soon became apparent that many businesses would need a combination of different applications. A typical business might require a word processor for correspondence, a spreadsheet for numerical work and a database to help keep track of information such as names and addresses.

As the price of personal computing hardware fell, purchasers were seen to be reluctant to spend large sums on software. To purchase a leading trio of applications could cost almost as much as the computer hardware itself. It was also realised that many first-time computer users did not want to spend long periods of time learning how to use different programs.

These factors resulted in the development of integrated programs. The aim was to create *one* program that was capable of performing *all* the functions of the separate applications. The real benefit is that data can be moved from application to application easily so, for example, data can be processed in a spreadsheet, then the spreadsheet can be included in a word processed report.

Section 2

The market for integrated packages has grown steadily with most major software houses having one, eg MS Works, Lotus Works, Ability, Framework, Mini-Office and Claris Works.

With the advent of the Windows interface the ability to transfer information between applications is much easier and so some of the advantages of integrated packages have lessened. Some software companies are now packaging up a spreadsheet, database and word processing program into a single, more economical product, eg Microsoft are offering a trio of Excel, Access and Word (all windows versions) which is known collectively as Office.

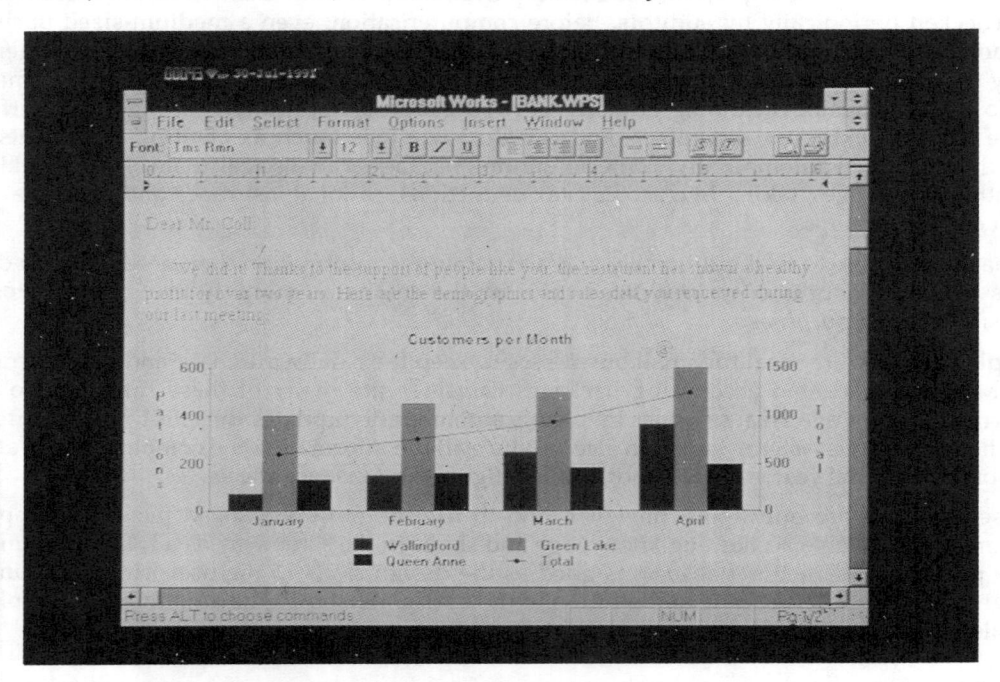

An integrated package, such as MS Works, makes it easy to incorporate text and spreadsheet graphs in the same document.

17.2 Choosing integrated software

Most integrated packages are based primarily around one particular function. They may, for instance, have a particularly well-specified spreadsheet, or they may have a more powerful database. When selecting a program you must check that its strengths match your needs.

No integrated package is going to be as powerful as a dedicated single program and it is important for users to understand this. It might well be better, for instance, for a business that is looking to use the computer mainly for correspondence to purchase a powerful word processor, rather than an integrated package.

Not all integrated packages allow for easy transfer of information from one function to another, so you must ensure that the procedures involved are ones that you are happy with.

Some integrated packages do not have common methods of control within the functions and so there may not be as much time saved in learning to use them as might have been hoped for.

Unit 18 Musical instrument digital interface

All data that is processed by computer is digital, that is it consists of a combination of 0s and 1s (known as binary numbers), with the 0s being represented by low voltages, and the 1s being represented by high voltages. Therefore, if a computer is going to be used to process data then that data must be in binary form. Once the information is in this format, however, the computer is able to do many things with it.

In this way the Musical Instrument Digital Interface, or MIDI, was developed. This is a standard that allows musical information, such as the pitch and length of a note, to be changed into a digital format that the computer can use. Equally, the computer's digital information can be translated into a form that a suitable instrument, for example a keyboard, could use. To be able to do this computers must have a MIDI converter, or interface, attached to them. This interface will allow the computer and a MIDI instrument (or instruments) to communicate.

To ensure that the instrument plays the correct notes in the correct order, or sequence, the computer will have to run a program called a *sequencer*. It is through the sequencer that the instrument will be controlled.

There are many advantages to using a computer when producing music. Since the computer can both store and process the MIDI information, work can be carried out on the music *separately* from the actual playing of the instrument. Thus it is possible to change the speed of playing, change any wrong notes or get the computer to move the notes from one part of the composition to another.

However, as the technology has advanced a number of other features have been developed. The vast majority of MIDI instruments are now able to play a number of notes at one time (called *polyphonic)* and can also play different sounds at one time (called *multi-timbral*). With these types of instrument one could have, say, a drum sequence playing *and*, on the same instrument and at the same time, have a synthesiser sound playing. Different MIDI instruments can have different numbers of notes playing at one time and also different numbers of sounds, or voices. So, a 16 note polyphonic instrument can play up to 16 notes at the same time whereas a 32 note polyphonic can play up to 32 notes at the same time. Similarly, a four-voice multi-timbral instrument can play four different sounds at the same time, whereas an eight-voice multi-timbral instrument can play eight different sounds at the same time.

With a suitable sequencer program running on a computer not only the notes of a composition can be controlled, but also the selection and sequencing of the voices of the instrument. It is therefore straightforward to experiment with different sounds to produce the desired effect.

Many sequencer programs can also carry out other functions. They can move the position of notes so that they match the tempo of the composition (called quantising) they may be able to display and print music in the standard stave format, or they may be able to transpose music from one key to another.

Since MIDI allows devices to communicate it is possible to link more than one MIDI device to a computer running a sequencer programme so one could have, for instance, a drum machine and two keyboards all being controlled by one computer. For this to happen the interface, and perhaps the devices, has to have *MIDI in*, *MIDI out* and *MIDI thru'* ports. The *in* port accepts MIDI signals, the *out* port sends MIDI signals and the *thru'* port allows the MIDI signals to be passed along without changing or being changed.

Each section of MIDI information is called a track. Normally MIDI only allows for 16 tracks but many sequencer programs can handle 32 or even 64 tracks. This is to allow them either to control

Section 2

more than one MIDI device, or to allow for different MIDI voices and parts of compositions to be on individual tracks.

It is important to realise, however, that whatever features a sequencer program has it does not replace the imagination and skill needed to produce pleasing and exciting compositions.

Unit 19 Further information technology applications

19.1 Introduction

The development of cheap, small, reliable but powerful microprocessors has resulted in an explosion of information technology applications. There are few aspects of our lives that have not been touched or changed by the small silicon chip.

19.2 Business

In the last decade the business world has been revolutionised by the development of small desktop microcomputers running a vast array of software. This software is very sophisticated and powerful and enables office workers at all levels to improve their efficiency and productivity. Word processing software has replaced typewriters as the essential clerical tool, database software has radically changed the way files and records are stored, spreadsheet software has drastically improved the monitoring of financial transactions in a business. Other software, such as desktop publishing and graphics, has also improved the way businesses can prepare documents and files, improving their corporate image. Such software has not only made businesses more productive and efficient but has also changed the working patterns of today's modern office.

The application of microprocessors is not restricted to computers but has also been applied to other office equipment and can be found controlling sophisticated photocopiers, electronic typewriters and pocket calculators. Large copiers are now available that can print double sided paper, collate, staple documents, shrink and expand images and produce them in high-quality colour. All aspects of the modern office have been affected and this has resulted in an improved working environment with a smaller but more highly trained workforce.

19.3 Domestic

Within the home the microprocessor can be found in a wide range of equipment including audio and video equipment, cookers, microwave ovens, washing machines, cameras and digital watches. In addition, the appearance of the home computer, with its increasingly sophisticated software, provides today's homes with complex games, educational teaching aids and programs that encourage many forms of artistry ranging from the creation of computer graphics to the composition and arrangement of electronic music.

One of the first inexpensive word processors and printers (from Amstrad) which helped to popularise home computing

19.4 Education
Within schools and colleges education and training has changed considerably with the introduction of computers. Within schools programs have been developed which help children to recognise numbers and letters and provide alternative teaching methods for different subject areas. Colleges and universities also use computers for vocational training and as an open access tool for students to prepare their work.

19.5 Arts
In the art world the microprocessor has enabled the development of synthesised music, highly developed computer animation and realistic computer graphics.

19.6 Defence
In the Armed Forces, complex weapons systems have been developed which offer the modern army, navy and airforce a formidable array of weaponry, guided missile and battle management systems. All modern warships, aircraft, submarines and battle tanks have on-board computers to help with navigation and military communications.

19.7 Police
The establishment of the Police National Computer at Hendon, which links large mainframe regional computers with one another and with other international policing agencies, has resulted in a far more coordinated approach to solving crimes and preventing acts of terrorism.

Section 2

An Apple Macintosh Colour Classic being used with an educational package for young children

19.8 Highstreet

Highstreet shops are increasingly using computerised point-of-sale terminals which produce itemised receipts and send details of a sale to a central computer to be is used for stock control and sales analysis.

Banks and building societies have installed cash dispensers throughout their branches, providing customers with instant access to their bank accounts 24 hours a day. They also provide a fast cheque clearing process, credit card facilities, and electronic transfer of funds, all of which would not have been possible without the development of the microprocessor.

Section 3 Skills bank

This section includes exercises which are to be used in conjunction with Section 1 scenarios. These exercises are broken down into the four skill areas of wordprocessing, database, spreadsheet and graphics. They are intended to be used as introductory exercises that will provide you with necessary skills to tackle the problems within the Section 1 units.

Systems notes

The system notes sections at the end of each block of exercises provide you with space to record the various commands that the system you are currently using requires in order to carry out a particular task.

They should be used in conjunction with the appropriate skills building exercises and those units in Secion 1 requiring practical use of software. The blank pages of the 'notes' can be used to record operating and safety or security procedures.

You should build up your systems notes gradually as you are asked to do different tasks. This information can be gained from consulting both computer software manuals and by talking to your lecturer or teacher. Completion of your notes will provide you with a source of reference for the future.

Example of how the notes should be used.

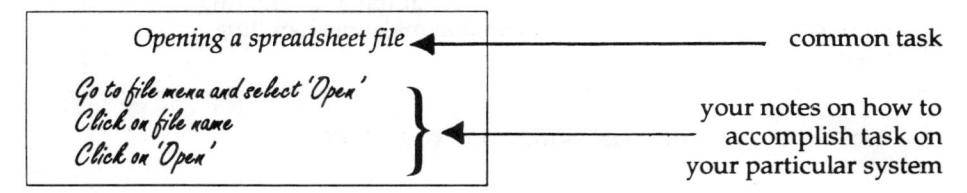

Opening a spreadsheet file ← common task

Go to file menu and select 'Open'
Click on file name ← your notes on how to accomplish task on your particular system
Click on 'Open'

Contents

- Word processing exercises *106*
- Word processing systems notes *115*
- Spreadsheet exercises *118*
- Spreadsheet systems notes *125*
- Database exercises *129*
- Database systems notes *135*
- Graphics exercises *138*
- Graphics systems notes *144*

Section 3

Unit 1 Word processing skills building

In this exercise you will create, enter, print and save a document.

Using your word processor, carry out the following tasks:

Task 1 Create a new document to be called *WORDPRO.EX1*.

Task 2 Check that the margins are correct.

Task 3 Enter the following text with single line spacing:

> Word processing is the facility to use a computer to input, edit, store and print out text. Using the computer for this offers many advantages, including ease of correction, space saving on storage and the option to use text enhancements. Text enhancement is the ability that word processors have to instruct printers to alter the way text is displayed. These enhancements can include emboldening which makes the text thicker, underlining which places a line under the chosen text and italicisation which slants the text to the right. Word processing also offers the opportunity for automatic centering of lines of text and many other features that make the handling of text easier.

Task 4 Save the document to your disk, using the name *WORDPRO.EX1*.

Task 5 Print out one copy of your work.

Remember to complete your system notes.

Then return to Section 1.

Unit 2 Word processing skills building

In this exercise you will recall, edit (using emboldening, underlining and italicisation), print and save a document.

Task 1 Recall the document *WORDPRO.EX1* for editing.

Task 2 Make the following changes to it:
- Replace 'print out' with 'reproduce'.
- Change 'many advantages, including ease', to 'many advantages. These include ease'.
- Change the sentence starting 'These enhancements', using the text enhancements so that it matches the following sentence:

> These enhancements can include **emboldening** which makes the text thicker, <u>underlining</u> which places a line under the chosen text and *italicisation* which slants the text to the right.

Task 3 Save this document as *WORDPRO.EX2*.

Task 4 Print out one copy of your document.

Section 3

Unit 3 Word processing skills building

In this exercise you will recall, edit, print and save a document.

Task 1   Recall your document *WORDPRO.EX2*.

Task 2   Use your cursor and return key to insert blank lines and create separate paragraphs:

> Word processing is the facility to use a computer to input, edit, store and reproduce text. Using the computer for this offers many advantages.
>
> These include ease of correction, space saving on storage and the ability to use text enhancements. Text enhancement is the ability that word processors have to instruct printers to alter the way text is displayed.
>
> These enhancements can include **emboldening** which makes the text thicker, underlining which places a line under the chosen text and *italicisation* which slants the text to the right.
>
> Word processing also offers the opportunity for automatic centering of lines of text and many other features that make the handling of text easier.

Task 3   Save your document as *WORDPRO.EX3*.

Task 4   Print out one copy of your document.

Unit 4 Word processing skills building

In this exercise you will recall, edit (setting specified justification and line spacing), print and save a document.

Task 1   Recall your document *WORDPRO.EX3*

Task 2   Using centering, right justification, 1½ line spacing and text enhancement features, edit your document so it matches the following:

WORD PROCESSING

Word processing is the facility to use a computer to input, edit, store and reproduce text. Using the computer for this offers many advantages.

These include ease of correction, space saving on storage and the ability to use text enhancements. Text enhancement is the ability that word processors have to instruct printers to alter the way text is displayed.

These enhancements can include **emboldening** which makes the text thicker, underlining which places a line under the chosen text and *italicisation* which slants the text to the right.

Word processing also offers the opportunity for automatic centering of lines of text and many other features that make the handling of text easier.

Many word processors also allow for the use of different styles of typeface, these different styles are often referred to as **fonts**. Depending on which word processor and which printer are being used it is possible to change fonts within the same document.

Task 3   Save your document as *WORDPRO.EX4*.

Task 4   Print one copy of your document.

Section 3

Unit 5 Word processing skills building

In this exercise you will recall, edit (cutting and pasting portions of text), print and save your document.

Task 1   Recall your document *WORPRO.EX4*.

Task 2   Using the cut and paste feature of your word processor edit your document to rearrange the last two paragraphs:

> ### WORD PROCESSING
>
> Word processing is the facility to use a computer to input, edit, store and reproduce text. Using the computer for this offers many advantages.
>
> These include ease of correction, space saving on storage and the ability to use text enhancements. Text enhancement is the ability that word processors have to instruct printers to alter the way text is displayed.
>
> These enhancements can include **emboldening** which makes the text thicker, underlining which places a line under the chosen text and *italicisation* which slants the text to the right.
>
> Many word processors also allow for the use of different styles of typeface, these different styles are often referred to as **fonts**. Depending on which word processor and which printer are being used it is possible to change fonts within the same document.
>
> Word processing also offers the opportunity for automatic centering of lines of text and many other features that make the handling of text easier.

Task 3   Save your document as *WORPRO.EX5*.

Task 4   Print one copy of your document.

Remember to complete your system notes.
Then return to Section 1.

Unit 6 Word processing skills building

In this exercise you will set up and use suitable tabs, save and print your document.

Task 1 Using your word processor's *tabulation* feature set one tab at 4 inches (102 mm).

Task 2 Using this tab, centering and emboldening, copy the memo that is shown below. Line spacing should be set to single line spacing and the right margin should be ragged.

> **MEMORANDUM**
>
> FROM: Sales Director   TO: Sales Staff
>
> DATE: 18th March 1993   RE: Sales Campaign
>
> As you must be aware the company will be launching a major sales campaign over the next two months. This campaign will be concentrating on stimulating interest in our latest products. The campaign will focus particularly on the new **Super Widget** and also our improved **Automatic Binder**.
>
> The campaign will be mainly concentrated on the usual trade papers but will be supported by direct mailings to our existing customers. It is important that you are aware of the following special offers being made during the campaign:
>
> **Super Widgets**   **10% OFF**
>
> **Automatic Binders**   **25% OFF**
>
> With these offers and the support of an extensive campaign you should be aiming for new record sales.

Task 3 Save your document as *WORDPRO.EX6*.

Task 4 Print one copy of your document.

Task 5 Check that it is correct and edit if required, saving and printing again.

Section 3

Unit 7 Word processing skills building

In this exercise you will recall, edit, (using the search and replace function) save and print your document.

Task 1 — Recall the document *WORDPRO.EX6* for editing

Task 2 — The company has decided to change the name of the **Super Widget** to the **Supreme Widget**. Using the search and replace function of your word processor, replace all occurrences of **Super Widget** with **Supreme Widget**.

Task 3 — The company has also decided to change the name of the **Automatic Binder** to **Binder Deluxe**. Using the search and replace function make the appropriate changes to your document.

Task 4 — Save your document, on your disk, as *WORDPRO.EX7*.

Task 5 — Print one copy of your document.

Task 6 — Proof read your document and if required edit, save and print again.

Unit 8 Word processing skills building

In this exercise you will create a new document, use a variety of tab settings, use a variety of text enhancements, use specified justification and line spacing, save and print your document.

Task 1   Open a new document.

Task 2   Using the tabulation feature set left tabs at 1.5, 4, and 5 inches (38, 102 and 127mm). Also set a right tab at 6 inches (152mm).

Task 3   Using the tabs and text enhancements as required, with single line spacing and the right margin ragged, enter the letter on the following page.

Task 4   Save your document, to your disk, as *WORDPRO.EX8*.

Task 5   Print one copy of your document.

Task 6   Proof read your document and if required edit, save and print again.

Remember to complete your system notes.

Then return to Section 1.

113

12 Highstreet
Anytown
Shire
SH4 KL5

19th April 1993

Humphrey Supplies
Alston Lane
NAUGHTON
Cleveland
CH3 7DT

Dear Sir

As requested here is a list of the different destinations to which we deliver and the days that we deliver on. I have also provided details of whether the deliveries are likely to be A.M. or P.M. I must emphasise that these are for **guidance only** and *no guarantee* is given or implied.

AREA	DAY	TIME
Brotton	Mon	AM
Saltburn	Mon	PM
Guisborough	Tue	AM
Redcar	Tue	PM
Middlesborough	Wed	AM
Stockton	Wed	PM
Darlington	Thur	AM
Durham	Thur	PM
Easington	Fri	AM
Chester-le-Street	Fri	PM

I trust you find the above useful and would be happy to assist you should you wish to contact me.
Yours sincerely

Margaret Hogan
Transport Manager

Word processing systems notes

File handling

Creating a word processed document	Opening an existing document

Saving a document	Printing a document

Text enhancement

Underlining text	Emboldening text

Italic text	Subscript

Superscript	Shadow

Outline	Strike through

Text alignment

Right align	Left align

Section 3

Centre	Justify
Setting tabs	Setting margins

Other

Insert page break	Title page
Set header	Set footer
Find text	Search and replace text
Cut text	Copy text
Paste text	Move text
Delete text	

Your own notes

Section 3

Unit 9 Spreadsheet skills building

In this exercise you will enter numeric and text data.

Task 1 Create a new spreadsheet file and enter the following data:

	A	B	C
1	NAME	RATE OF PAY	HOURS WORKED
2	ADAMS	£3.75	37
3	BROWN	£3.25	37
4	COLLINS	£4.50	37
5	HORNE	£4.00	37
6	JACKSON	£3.75	37
7	MORRIS	£5.25	37
8	PERCY	£4.50	37
9	ROBERTS	£3.75	37
10	STACY	£3.25	37
11	WILSON	£4.00	37

Create your own system notes on how to enter and display data.
Refer to manuals or lecturers.

Task 2 Save and print one copy of your spreadsheet.

Unit 10 Spreadsheet skills building

In this exercise you will enter a multiplication formula to calculate gross pay, and to enter a formula to calculate totals.

Task 1   Open your wages spreadsheet file and enter a formula that will calulate Gross pay. (Tip: multiply 'RATE OF PAY' with 'HOURS WORKED'.)

	A	B	C	D
1	NAME	RATE OF PAY	HOURS WORKED	GROSS PAY
2	ADAMS	£3.75	37	insert formula
3	BROWN	£3.25	37	insert formula
4	COLLINS	£4.50	37	insert formula
5	HORNE	£4.00	37	insert formula
6	JACKSON	£3.75	37	insert formula
7	MORRIS	£5.25	37	insert formula
8	PERCY	£4.50	37	insert formula
9	ROBERTS	£3.75	37	insert formula
10	STACY	£3.25	37	insert formula
11	WILSON	£4.00	37	insert formula
12	TOTAL			insert formula

Insert a formula to total gross pay column.

Task 2   Save your spreadsheet as *WAGES 2* and print one copy.

Remember to complete your system notes.

Then return to Section 1.

Section 3

Unit 11 Spreadsheet skills building

In this exercise you will enter a multiplication formula to calculate tax due.

Task 1 Open your *WAGES 2* spreadsheet file and enter a formula that will calulate TAX DUE. (Tip: Multiply GROSS PAY by .25. See your systems notes for help.)

	A	B	C	D	E
1	NAME	RATE OF PAY	HOURS WORKED	GROSS PAY	TAX DUE
2	ADAMS	£3.75	37	£138.75	insert formula
3	BROWN	£3.25	37	£120.25	insert formula
4	COLLINS	£4.50	37	£166.50	insert formula
5	HORNE	£4.00	37	£148.00	insert formula
6	JACKSON	£3.75	37	£138.75	insert formula
7	MORRIS	£5.25	37	£194.25	insert formula
8	PERCY	£4.50	37	£166.50	insert formula
9	ROBERTS	£3.75	37	£138.75	insert formula
10	STACY	£3.25	37	£120.25	insert formula
11	WILSON	£4.00	37	£148.00	insert formula
12	TOTAL			£1480.00	insert formula

Insert a formula to total the TAX DUE column.

Task 2 Save your spreadsheet as *WAGES 3* and print one copy.

Unit 12 Spreadsheet skills building

In this exercise you will enter a minus formula to calculate total net pay.

Task 1 Open your *WAGES 3* spreadsheet file and enter a formula that will calulate NET PAY. (Tip: Subtract TAX DUE from GROSS PAY. See your systems notes for help.)

	A	B	C	D	E	F
1	NAME	RATE OF PAY	HOURS WORKED	GROSS PAY	TAX DUE	NET PAY
2	ADAMS	£3.75	37	£138.75	£34.69	insert formula
3	BROWN	£3.25	37	£120.25	£30.06	insert formula
4	COLLINS	£4.50	37	£166.50	£41.62	insert formula
5	HORNE	£4.00	37	£148.00	£37.00	insert formula
6	JACKSON	£3.75	37	£138.75	£34.69	insert formula
7	MORRIS	£5.25	37	£194.25	£48.56	insert formula
8	PERCY	£4.50	37	£166.50	£41.62	insert formula
9	ROBERTS	£3.75	37	£138.75	£34.69	insert formula
10	STACY	£3.25	37	£120.25	£30.06	insert formula
11	WILSON	£4.00	37	£148.00	£37.00	insert formula
12	TOTAL			£1480.00	£370.00	insert formula

Insert a formula to total the NET PAY column.

Task 2 Save your spreadsheet as *WAGES 4* and print one copy showing values and another showing formulae.

Remember to complete your system notes.
Then return to Section 1.

Section 3

Unit 13 Spreadsheet skills building

In this exercise you will create a simple invoice.

Task 1 Create a new spreadsheet file and enter the following data:

	A	B	C	D	E
1	Invoice				
2					
3	Ref	Quantity	Description	Unit cost	Extension
4	133	2	Acer LP76	£1300.00	insert formula
5	141	3	IBM 4216 Model 020	£1635.00	insert formula
6	175	8	Canon LBP 8iiT	£834.00	insert formula
7	170	1	Qume Scritpen	£1034.00	insert formula
8	135	1	Toshiba Pagelaser 12	£1833.00	insert formula
9	295	3	CITOH CL-5	£1956.00	insert formula
10	275	2	Sharp JX9300	£950.00	insert formula
11	223	2	Star Miconics LP8	£1278.00	insert formula
12				Sub Total	insert formula
13				VAT @ 17.5%	insert formula
14				Total Cost	insert formula
15					
16					

Use your system notes to enter a formula:
a) that will multiply the quantity with the total cost
b) to find the subtotal
c) to calculate VAT at 17.5%, and
d) to find the total cost including VAT.

Task 2 Save your spreadsheet as *INVOICE*.

Task 3 Print a copy of your spreadsheet.

Remember to complete your system notes.
Then return to Section 1.

Unit 14 Spreadsheets skills building – charts

The following exercises provide you with the opportunity to practise drawing charts using your spreadsheet and to discover the different commands and procedures that your spreadsheet uses to translate the numerical data on your spreadsheet into graphical information.

Task 1 Enter the following data into your spreadsheet and draw a bar chart:

*Figures showing the stocks of coal at Bankside colliery
July to December 1992*

Month	Total tonnage
July	7,729
August	8,171
September	8,456
October	11,230
November	11,412
December	11,749

Task 2 Enter the following data into your spreadsheet and draw a multi bar chart:

Figures comparing the production figures of a company manufacturing washing machines in the same period in two consecutive years.

	Jan	Feb	Mar	May	Jun
1991	40,564	37,123	43,654	51,734	60,213
1992	47,241	38,467	40,411	47,931	56,855

Task 3 Enter the following data into your spreadsheet and draw a line graph showing sales figures for softwood:

Month	figures (000 cubic metres)	Month	figures (000 cubic metres)
January	432	July	845
February	568	August	582
March	629	September	700
April	578	October	845
May	732	November	811
June	723	December	622

Section 3

Task 4 Enter the following figures and create a pie chart showing weekly household expenditure for a single person in 1989:

Item	£
Rent	36.00
Fuel	12.00
Food	37.00
Clothing	15.00
Car	18.00
Alcohol	10.00

Task 5 Enter the following data and create a multi stack chart showing a breakdown of age distribution in a company called Lascos over the last three years:

Year	Under 25	25-45	45-60	60 and over
1990	18	12	15	5
1991	23	14	11	2
1992	26	16	7	1

Remember to complete your system notes.

Then return to Section 1.

Spreadsheet systems notes

File handling

Creating a new spreadsheet	Opening an existing spreadsheet
Saving a spreadsheet	Printing a spreadsheet

Formulae

Adding numbers in cells	Subtracting numbers in cells
Dividing numbers in cells	Multiplying numbers in cells
Adding a range of cells	Finding the average of a range of cells
Calculating percentages	

Cell format

Right align	Left align

Section 3

Centre	*Underline*
Embolden	*Change column width*
Set numeric attribute	*Set text attribute*
Delete data	*Copy data*
Paste data	*Move data*
Replicate data	*Show values*
Show formulae	*Protect data*
Unprotect data	*Insert row*
Insert column	*Delete row*

Spreadsheet systems notes

Delete column

Charts

Creating a pie chart	Creating a bar chart
Creating a line graph	Creating a stack chart
Saving charts	Printing charts

Section 3

Your own notes

Unit 15 Database skills building

In this exercise you will define the fields of a simple personnel database file that will keep track of employees' holidays. You will enter the data, sort the data alphabetically and numerically, generate and print a report and save the database file.

Task 1 Create a database file that has the following fields:

Field name	Field specification
SURNAME	– An alphabetic field of up to 15 characters in length.
FORENAME	– An alphabetic field of up to 10 characters in length
DEPARTMENT	– An alphabetic field of up to eight characters in length
HOLIDAYS	– A numeric field of up to three characters in length.

Task 2 Enter the data on the following page into the database file. **N.B.** The following abbreviations should be used for the **DEPARTMENT**:

   Admin (Administration),

   Prod (Production) and

   Trans (Transport).

Task 3 Save your database file as *PERS1DB*.

Task 4 Print a report of your database file entitled 'Report One'.

Task 5 Sort your database file into alphabetical order by SURNAME and print a report entitled 'Surname Report'.

Task 6 Sort the file into ascending numerical order by HOLIDAYS and print a report entitled Holidays Report.

Task 7 Re-save your database file as *PERS2DB*.

Remember to complete your system notes.
Then return to Section 1.

Section 3

SURNAME	FORENAME	DEPARTMENT	HOLIDAYS
Bowsley	Terence	Admin	2
Horan	Tessa	Admin	5
Harris	Martin	Trans	3
Williams	David	Prod	8
Lowe	Mary	Trans	6
Murphy	Adam	Prod	3
Anderson	Ann	Trans	12
Aspinall	Maria	Prod	13
Macintosh	James	Admin	10
Thompson	Richard	Prod	5
Jones	Sian	Trans	8
Smith	Anna	Prod	9
Carter	Joesph	Admin	12
Smith	Andrew	Prod	14
Hayes	Peter	Prod	8
Daley	Jonathan	Trans	4
Evans	William	Prod	5
Franks	John	Prod	9
Preston	Patrick	Prod	2
Blackburn	Arthur	Trans	4
Burton	Francis	Admin	6
Yeats	Rebecca	Prod	7
Hinds	Robert	Admin	12
Locke	Peter	Prod	10
Newsam	Stephen	Trans	5
Orr	Elaine	Prod	11
Owen	Margaret	Trans	10
Parkin	Teresa	Prod	4
Potter	Fredrick	Admin	12
Ellis	Peter	Prod	6
Rix	Dean	Prod	12
Rogers	Paul	Prod	11

Unit 16 Database skills building

In this exercise you will recall an existing database file, edit data in the fields and re-save the database file.

Task 1 Open the database file entitled *PERS2DB* created in Unit 15.

Task 2 Using the data below, make the following changes to the employees' holidays field:

the following staff have taken *additional* holidays which need to be added to their existing totals:

SURNAME	FORENAME	HOLIDAYS
Blackburn	Arthur	5
Bowsley	Terence	3
Daley	Jonathan	4
Preston	Patrick	10
Parkin	Teresa	5
Murphy	Adam	4
Harris	Martin	6

Task 3 Make the following changes to the employees' SURNAME field:

The following surnames need to be changed:

Horan, Tessa becomes Bryant, Tessa

Smith, Anna becomes Dorkins, Anna

Task 4 Make the following changes to the employees' DEPARTMENT field:

the following staff are now in new departments:

SURNAME	FORENAME	DEPARTMENT
Smith	Andrew	Trans
Newsam	Stephen	Prod

Task 5 Save your database file as *PERS3DB*.

Section 3

Unit 17 Database skills building

In this exercise you will open an existing database file, insert a new field, insert data, re-save the database file, sort the file numerically and generate and print reports.

Task 1   Open the database file entitled *PERS3DB* created in the previous exercise.

Task 2   Add a new field entitled SICKNESS – a numeric field, maximum of three characters in length.

Task 3   Add another new field entitled OCCURRENCE – a numeric field, maximum of three characters in length.

Task 4   Enter the data on the following page into the SICKNESS and OCCURRENCE fields.

Task 5   Save your database file as *PERS4DB*.

Task 6   Sort your database file into descending numerical order by SICKNESS and print a report entitled Sickness Report.

Task 7   Sort your database file into ascending numerical order by OCCURRENCE and print a report entitled Occurrence Report.

Task 8   Re-Save your database file as *PERS4DB*.

Remember to complete your system notes.

Then return to Section 1.

Unit 17: Database skills building

SURNAME	FORENAME	SICKNESS	OCCURRENCE
Bowsley	Terence	2	1
Bryant	Tessa	4	1
Harris	Martin	9	2
Williams	David	5	1
Lowe	Mary	7	1
Murphy	Adam	3	2
Anderson	Ann	1	1
Aspinall	Maria	0	0
Macintosh	James	0	0
Thompson	Richard	4	2
Jones	Sian	7	3
Dorkins	Anna	6	1
Carter	Joesph	3	1
Smith	Andrew	12	5
Hayes	Peter	5	2
Daley	Jonathan	4	1
Evans	William	5	1
Franks	John	0	0
Preston	Patrick	0	0
Blackburn	Arthur	0	0
Burton	Francis	0	0
Yeats	Rebecca	8	2
Hinds	Robert	4	1
Locke	Peter	0	0
Newsam	Stephen	3	2
Orr	Elaine	2	2
Owen	Margaret	1	1
Parkin	Teresa	0	0
Potter	Fredrick	0	0
Ellis	Peter	8	3
Rix	Dean	3	3
Rogers	Paul	2	1

Section 3

Unit 18 Database skills building

In this exercise you will recall a database file, interrogate the database file using selection criteria, generate and print reports and re-save the database file.

Task 1   Open the database file entitled *PERS4DB* created in the last exercise. Interrogate the file to select all those staff who have had more than ten days holiday. Print a report of your findings.

Task 2   Interrogate the file to select all those staff who have had more than three occurrences of illness. Print a report of your findings.

Task 3   Interrogate the file to select all those staff who have had over eight days sickness. Print a report of your findings.

Task 4   Interrogate the file to select all those staff in the production department who have had less than ten days holiday. Print a report of your findings.

Task 5   Interrogate the file to select all those staff in the transport department who have had less than twelve days holiday. Print a report of your findings.

Task 6   Interrogate the file to select all those staff in the production department who have had more than four days sickness. Print a report of your findings.

Task 7   Interrogate the file to select all those staff who have had more than eight days sickness *or* more than twelve days holiday. Print a report of your findings.

Task 8   Interrogate the file to select all those staff who have had more than eight days sickness *or* more than two occurrencies of illness. Print a report of your findings.

Task 9   Re-save your file as *PERS4DB*.

Remember to complete your system notes.

Then return to Section 1.

Database systems notes

File handling

Creating a new database	*Opening an existing database*
Saving a database	*Creating a report*

Setting attributes or formats of fields

Text format	*Numeric format*
Fixed numbers	*Currency numbers*
Percentage numbers	*Scientific numbers*
Date format	*Time format*

Other

Right align	*Left align*

Section 3

Centre	*Underline*
Embolden	*Change field width*
Delete a record	*Add a record*
Copy a record	*Paste a record*
Move a record	*Insert a record*

Your own notes

Section 3

Unit 19 Graphics skills building

In this exercise you will practise using the line tool on your graphics package to create simple triangles.

Task 1   Draw the following triangles and print one copy.

(a)

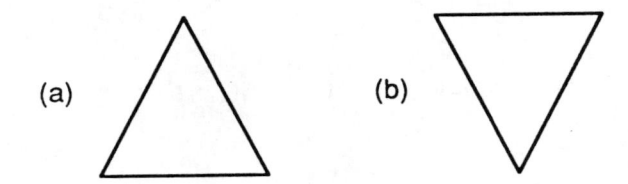

(b)

Task 2   Draw the following triangles and print one copy.

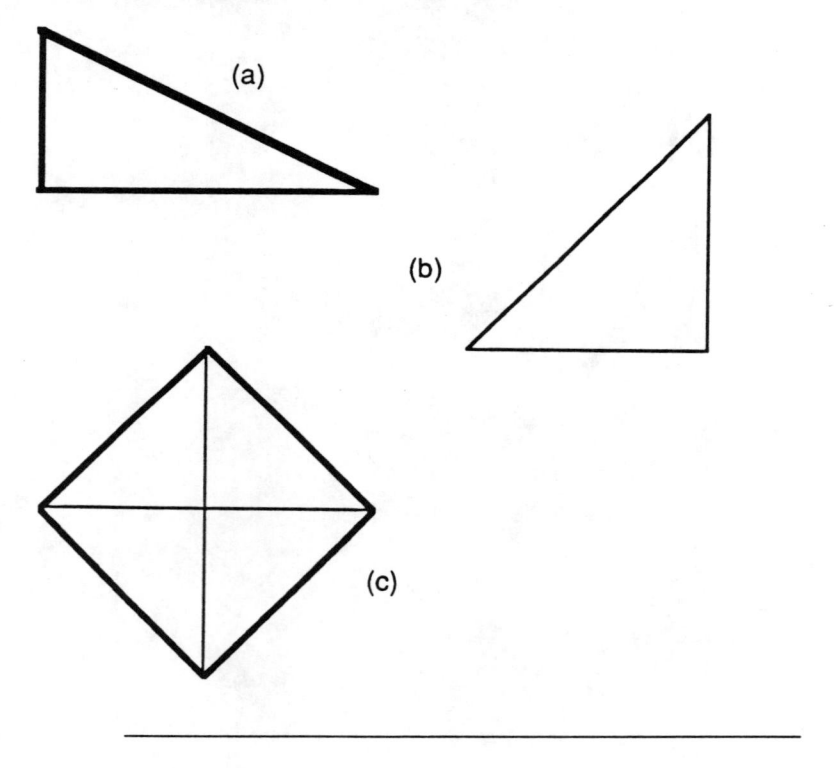

(a)

(b)

(c)

Unit 20 Graphics skills building

In this exercise you will practise using the 'square' tool on your graphics package to create simple squares and rectangles with different fill patterns.

Task 1 Draw the following squares and rectangles.

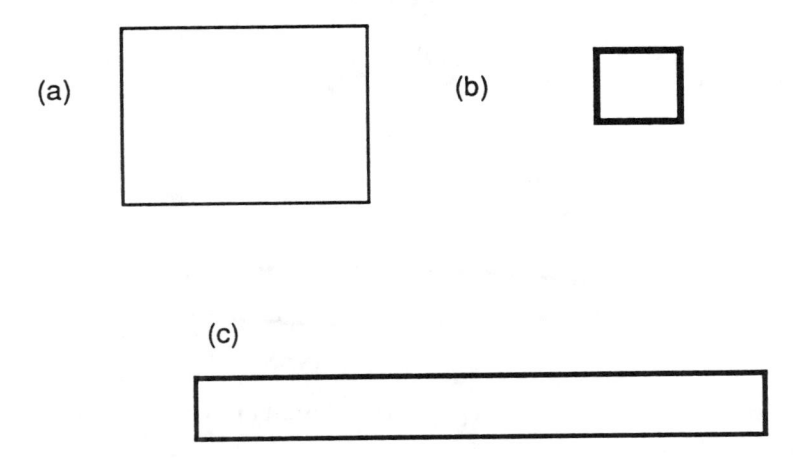

(a)

(b)

(c)

Task 2 Draw the following shapes. Include a fill pattern and print one copy.

(a)

(b)

(c)

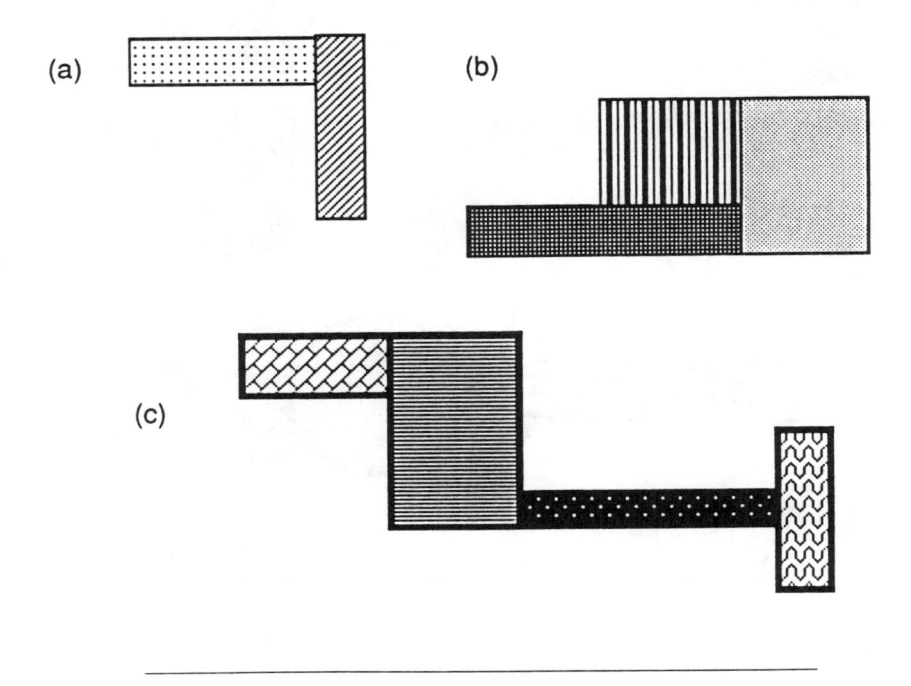

139

Section 3

Unit 21 Graphics skills building

In this exercise you will practise using the circle tool on your graphics package to create simple circles and elipses with fill patterns.

Task 1   Draw the following circles and elipses and print one copy.

(a)

(b)

(c)

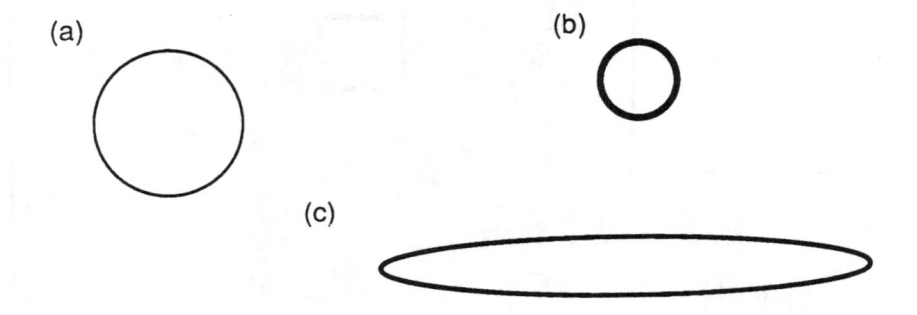

Task 2   Draw the following shapes, include fill patterns and print one copy.

(a)

(b)

(c)

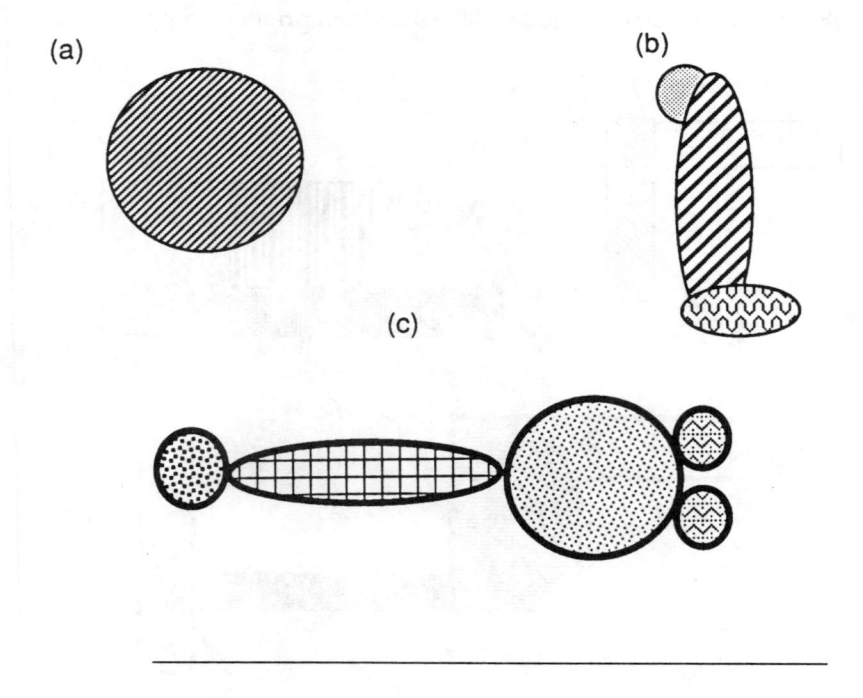

140

Unit 22 Graphics skills building

In this exercise you will practise creating labels.

Task 1 Draw the following shapes using your round-cornered square tool.

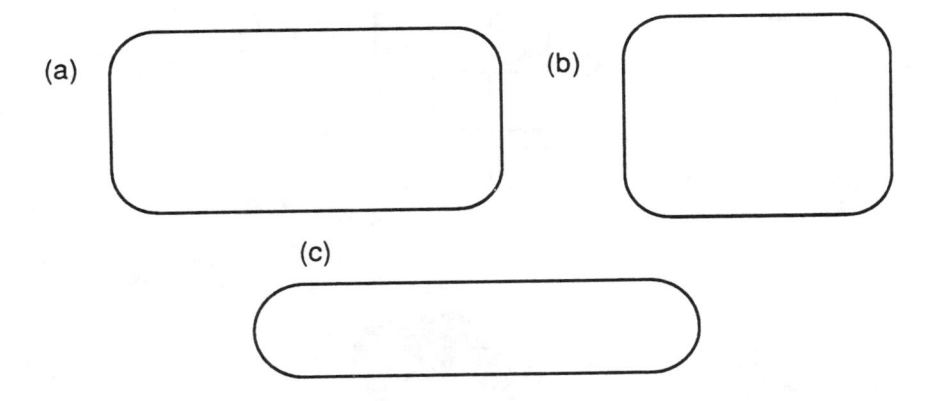

(a)

(b)

(c)

Task 2 Now place the following text inside the shape and use a fill pattern to decorate the inside of the shape.

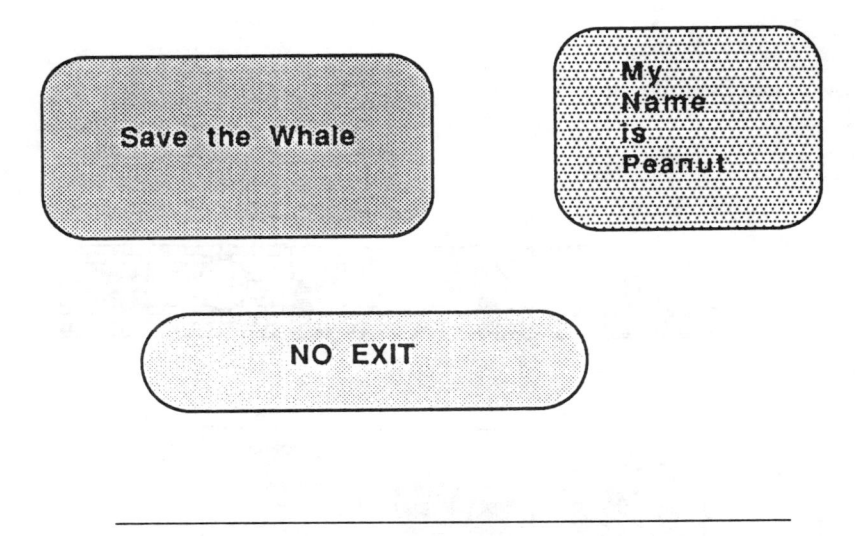

Save the Whale

My Name is Peanut

NO EXIT

141

Section 3

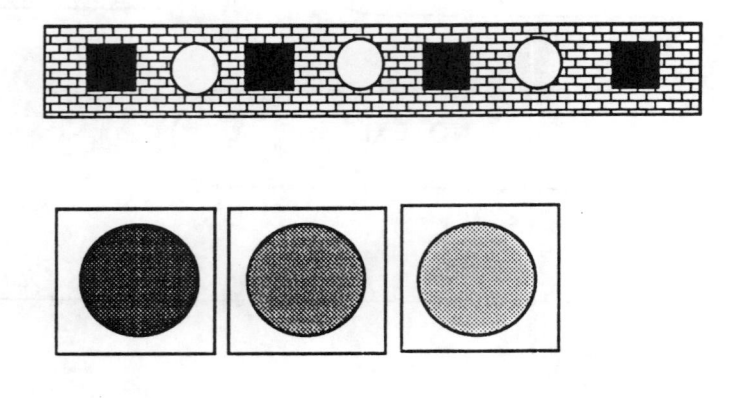

Unit 23 Graphics skills building

In this exercise you will practise using your copy and paste function to create and duplicate shapes.

Task 1 Draw the following shapes and use the copy and paste function to make duplicates.

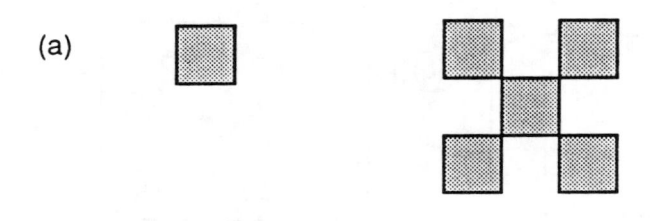

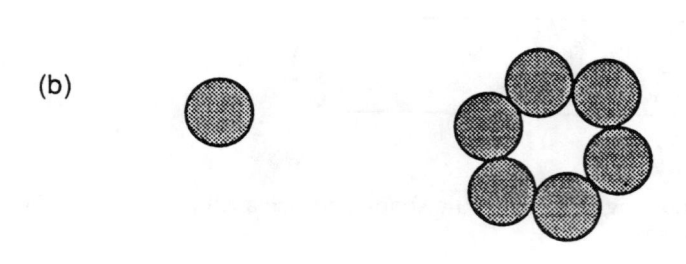

(a)

(b)

Task 2 Now create the following.

(a)

Unit 24: Graphics skills building

Unit 24 Graphics skills building

In this exercise you will use the skills and techniques you have acquired to create the images below.

Task 1   Create the following picture:

Task 2   Now create the following.

Remember to complete your system s notes .
Then return to Section 1

Section 3

Graphics systems notes

Opening a new file	Drawing a straight line
Drawing a triangle	Drawing a square
Rotating	Filling
Copying	Drawing ellipses

Your own notes

Spreadsheet systems notes

Section 4 Assignments

This section contains seven assignments that you may be set by your teacher/lecturer as part of your assessment.

Contents
1   Buying a computer *148*
2   Communications *149*
3   Evaluating equipment *150*
4   IT in the business environment *151*
5   Word processing *152*
6   Spreadsheets *154*
7   Databases *155*

Assignments

1 Buying a computer

Richard and Sarah have set up a small business called 'Stars and Stripes Footwear', buying fashionable footwear from America and selling it by mail order to retail outlets and customers in the UK. They have been trading for eight months and the business has proved to be very successful with students and teenagers who want the latest streetwear fashions straight from America.

They work from a small office and warehouse on the outskirts of Liverpool and conduct the majority of their business by post, sending catalogues and price lists to sport shops and mens' and womens' fashion shops. Occasionally they do get enquiries from individuals who ring them or actually appear at their office, but this is very rare.

Both of them have little experience of computers and, until now, they have been using an old computer that was given to them, to keep records of their customers, prepare letters and calculate payments and invoices.

One morning the computer refuses to work, it flashes up a systems error message and then the screen goes blank and will not respond to any of Sarah's efforts to revitalise it. Both Richard and Sarah are faced with the problem of replacing it. Flicking through the trade journals and browsing in shop windows confirms their suspicions that they are unprepared to face this task. They have very little knowledge of computers and are horrified at the thought of having to choose between computers which seem to be identical.

The advertisement below appears in a national computing trade journal listing six best selling features of a small personal computer system.

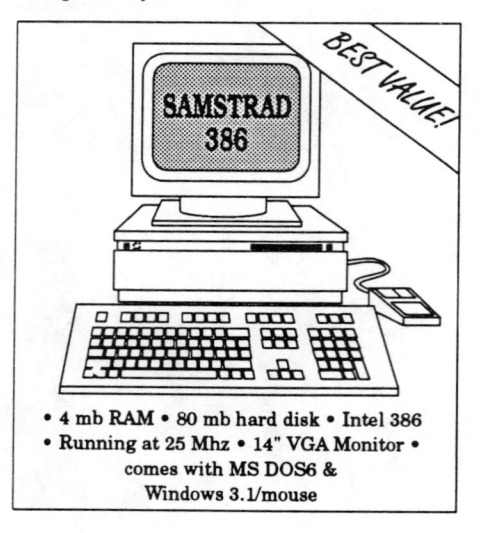

SAMSTRAD 386 — *BEST VALUE!*

- 4 mb RAM • 80 mb hard disk • Intel 386
- Running at 25 Mhz • 14" VGA Monitor •
  comes with MS DOS6 &
  Windows 3.1/mouse

Task   Study the advertisement above and write down an explanation of each one of the six features listed so that Richard and Sarah, who have little computer knowledge, are able to understand the advertisement.

2 Communications

There are many business organisations operating today that rely heavily upon the postal service to deliver vital business documents like order notes, advice notes, invoices and payments to suppliers and customers. While the British postal system offers an excellent customer service, with over 98% of first class letters being delivered the day after posting, any disruption to the service may result in important documents being delayed and business deals lost.

Mail order companies are particularly vulnerable should there be any disruption of services caused by Christmas surges of mail or industrial action by postal workers.

Equally, for many organisations the next day delivery is not fast enough, and many need instantaneous transmission of messages and business documents if they wish to compete successfully in today's economy. For these organisation alternative communication methods are necessary.

Task 1   Find out about alternative communication methods that could be used by a modern business for communicating with its customers and suppliers. Give a brief description of each service outlining their main advantages over the postal service.

Task 2   Write down a list of instructions, called a 'Users Guide', on how to use a facsimile machine, which could be used by anyone unfamiliar to the device.

Task 3   In groups examine an on-line database that you have access to and word process a description of the different information and customer services that it provides.

Assignments

3 Evaluating equipment

Within every organisation the pace of change in new technology is frantic; no sooner is an item of equipment purchased, unpacked and installed, than a new model which is faster, more efficient and offering a wider range of features appears on the market at a very competitive price.

It is easy to fall into the trap of wanting to buy the latest technology, but caution should be exercised so that buying decisions are made for sound practical reasons and not just to be fashionable. All computer hardware should be purchased to perform specific functions and meet ever changing user requirements. When the equipment can no longer meet those requirements or is unsuitable to perform those functions, then the equipment should be replaced or updated.

Task 1 The computer hardware that you are currently using was bought for a particular purpose and to satisfy a specific need. Look at the equipment and word process a description of the system hardware. This should include:

  a) the size of RAM available to the machine

  b) the type of microprocessor being used

  c) the different types of input device being used

  d) the different types of output device being used

  e) the type of backing storage being used

  f) the size and type of monitor being used.

Task 2 Examine the list of equipment that you have made and word process what you consider to be the strengths and weaknesses of each piece of equipment that you are currently using (keep in mind the purpose for which the equipment was bought).

Task 3 Word process a list of recommendations that will improve the equipment listed in Task 1, which would help overcome the weaknesses identified in Task 2. Such improvements may include either upgrading or totally replacing existing equipment. Where replacement of existing equipment is recommended, please specify accurately what it would be replaced with.

4 IT in the business environment

The versatility of information technology applications suggests that there is no business environment which has remained unaffected by the introduction of new technology. Information technology has radically changed the way people work in the modern office.

Task Examine the effects that the following information technology applications have had on the modern business office in the handling and processing of information:

a) Facsimile machine

b) Photocopier

c) Word processor

d) Electronic database

e) Pocket calculator

f) Spreadsheet

Your examination should include a description of working practices before and after the introduction of each of the above.

Assignments

5 Word processing

You are working in a business which has decided to appoint some additional trainee management staff. There has been one round of interviews already and there is now to be a selection conference for those applicants who proved successful in the first interviews. You arrive at work and find the following memo on your desk. Follow all the instructions and carry out the required tasks.

DRURIDGE PIPE COMPANY
Alsop Buildings
Mitre Trading Estate
Essex

MEMORANDUM

From: Alison Delund **To:** Personnel Assistant
Subject: Trainee Management Recruitment **Date:** 12/1/94

As you are no doubt aware, the first stage interviews were completed yesterday. We will be inviting the six candidates who have so far proved successful to the selection conference to be held here on the 12/2/94. The programme for the day will be as follows:

09:00	Arrival and coffee
09:15	Opening address – Ms. A. Delund, Recruitment Director
09:45	Sam the Van – Production Simulation
11:00	Coffee
11:15	Moonshot – group work exercise
12:30	Lunch
13:30	Field exercise briefing – Mr. D. Jones, Training Officer.
13:45	Field exercise planning Stage
14:15	Field exercise
16:00	Report stage
16:15	Tea
16:30	Individual interviews
17:30	Close

Could you please word process a suitable letter to the six applicants, details attached, inviting them to the selection conference. Make sure that you include details of the day's programme and all other necessary information. Ask the candidates to contact me on my direct number of 0245 65147 if they have any problem.

Thanks.

NAMES AND ADDRESSES OF CANDIDATES FOR
SELECTION CONFERENCE ON 12/2/94

Ms J. Johnson
14 Laburnum Drive
Halden
Middlesex
ME8 3TQ

Mr. K. Ogden
18 Dumbarton Road
Winslee
Essex
EX7 5LM

Mr. R. Hayes
256 Cumin Street
Aldersea
Shropshire
SH6 4WE

Mr. L. Barnes
1 The Grove
Barlas
Strathclyde
BZ4 9SK

Mrs. D. Katz
Mountlea
Tartlund
Cumbria
CU7 3AK

Ms. S. Farnworth
15 Cherry Crescent
Dimsley
Cornwall
CW6 1QT

Assignments

6 Spreadsheets

Task 1 Open a new spreadsheet document and create a spreadsheet from the figures given below which project a personal expenditure budget for the first six months of 1994. Save your spreadsheet as BUDGET. Print one copy.

The following revenue figures are projected for the first six months of 1994
    Salary   £947 per month

The following expenditure figures are projected for the first six months of 1994:
    Mortgage   £250 per month
    Electricity and heating   £110 per month
    Telephone   £35 per month
    Bank loan   £100 per month
    Insurance   £60 per month
    Car insurance   £35 per month
    Petrol   £80 per month
    Car tax   £120 in March
    AA membership   £12 per month
    Council tax   £48 per month

Task 2 Enter a formula below each column to calculate the total amount of money spent for each of the months January to June. Entitle the row 'Total spent'. Print one copy showing values.

Task 3 Add another row entitled 'Disposable income' that will calculate the amount of money that will be left once the total expenditure figures have been subtracted from the salary figures.

Task 4 Add an extra column after the June figures entitled 'Period Total'. Enter formulae in this column that will calculate the totals for the salary and each item of expenditure over the six month period. Print one copy showing values and one copy showing formulae.

Task 5 Suppose the car insurance was increased from £35.00 to £80.00 each month due to an insurance claim just after Christmas. Change the figures on your spreadsheet and print out one copy showing values only.

7 Databases

Richard and Sarah have made quite a number of contacts over the months. They have prepared a list of them, shown below. They would like the information to be transferred to a computerised database and then processed in a number of ways.

The information contains the name of the company, the person they are to contact, the address and phone number of the company and which type(s) of footwear each is interested in.

Sarah and Richard would like to be able to have separate lists, alphabetically sorted by:

- The companies, names
- The contacts, names
- The town or county

In addition they would like you to produce separate lists of which companies are interested in:

- Fashion footwear
- Sports footwear
- Special footwear

Task Transfer the information into a computerised database and then produce the separate print outs requested.

Sports Suppliers Ltd
12 Rockfield Lane
Hornfield
Essex IL3 3TR

Tel: 0605 234784

Contact: Harris J.

Interests: sports, special

Shoes For All
134 Houghton Road
Gateshead
Tyne and Wear NE9 8GH

Tel: 091 765 3902

Contact: McDonald K.

Interests: fashion

Western Shoes
234 Denton Burn
Hightown
Blackburn BL5 9YH

Tel: 0705 345 2839

Contact: Webster P.

Interests: sports, special, fashion

Direct Sports Supplies
4a Clayton Drive
Brunswick Industrial Estate
Merseyside L56 7TW

Tel: 051 637 5429

Contact: Harrap D.

Interests: sports, special

Assignments

Fashion Footwear
367 Raeburn Drive
Brixton
London SW2 7FD

Tel: 071 493 0320

Contact: Rogerson L.

Interests: fashion

Power Lifts
12 Randolph Crescent
Welfield
Shropshire SH2 9DQ

Tel: 0450 327 2901

Contact: Broughton T.

Interests: special, sports

AllSports
89 Freshfield Road
Fullerton
Bolton
Lancs B05 9FG

Tel: 0770 678 2081

Contact: Hill G.

Interests: sport

Browns Boots
192 Fetlock Way
Dilton
Birmingham BI3 7FA

Tel: 031 563 9583

Contact: Brown S.

Interests: fashion

Footloose Fashions
73 Hangar Hill Lane
Falkirk
Scotland FA3 6DS

Tel: 0620 790 2182

Contact: Andrews R.

Interests: fashion

Pedal Power
29 Front Street
Macclesfield
Cheshire MA8 9SW

Tel: 0920 726 8645

Contact: Dillon M.

Interests: sports, special

Clogs and Things
48 Welcome Lane
Tutworth
Devon EX7 4VR

Tel: 0392 703 3284

Contact: Season G.

Interests: fashion, special

Super Shoes
284 New Street
Axmouth
Devon EX3 7SJ

Tel: 0392 845 2115

Contact: Greaves H.

Interests: fashion, sports, special

Your Sports
75 Badger Rake
Hoylake
Merseyside L29 4DE

Tel: 051 723 2372

Contact: Bartlett L.

Interests: sports

Specialist sports Supplies
Unit 12 Dawpool Estate
Freshfields
Southport SO8 4FK

Tel: 0740 823 7345

Contact: Carr S.

Interests: special

Appendix – Answers to tasks in Section 1

Most tasks in Section 1 can be answered by following up the 'Help?' cross reference to information on that topic in Section 2 or to a Section 3 skills building exercises. A few tasks, however, require further analysis or calculation, and answers to these are included below.

Unit 1 Richard and Sarah Discover IT

Task 1

Receive orders customer name – alphabetic
customer address – alphanumeric
customer telephone number – numeric
description of goods ordered – alphabetic
quantity required – numeric
catalogue number – alphanumeric
date of order – alphanumeric
order note number – numeric

Invoices customer name – alphabetic
customer address – alphanumeric
customer order – alphanumeric
cost of goods – numeric
cost of VAT – numeric
cost of packaging – numeric
data of the order – alphanumeric
invoice note number – numeric

The calculation of invoices mainly involves numeric data, but as you can see above, for the invoice to be useful it has also to include alphabetic and alphanumeric data.

Stock records stock description – alphabetic
stock item number – alphanumeric
stock level – numeric

Maintaining stock levels requires all these data types.

Remittances customer name – alphabetic
customer address – alphanumeric
invoice number – numeric
cheque payment – alphanumeric
date – alphanumeric

Processing customer payments (remittances) involves handling cheques that contain a combination of alpha and numeric type data.

This exercise illustrates the fact that most everyday clerical activities involve processing data of all three types.

Appendix

Task 2

Job	Capture	Process	Store and retrieve	Communicate
Receive order	Completed order form	Check items in stock and create customer file	Keep a copy of order for records and file in logical place	No communication unless query on order. List orders taken to pass on for despatch
Prepare invoices	Completed order form or list of orders.	Calculate amount payable by customer	Keep a copy of invoice for records and file in logical place	Send copy of invoice to customer
Adjust stock levels	Completed order form or list of orders	Update stock lists by subtracting items ordered from stock held	Keep a copy of stock records and file in a logical place	Give details to person responsible for maintaining stock levels
Remittances	Cheque payment	Check amount received against customer invoice	Keep a record of payments received and file in a logical place	Acknowledgment of receipt of payment to customer. Enter customer payments into accounts

Unit 8 Looking after the finances

All figures are rounded to the nearest penny.

Task 1

Total cost is £165.96

Task 2

The total VAT is £29.04
the VAT and total price is as follows:

	VAT	Total
Slapshot	£7.52	£50.51
Super 9	£8.75	£58.74
Trident	£7.00	£46.99
Terminator	£8.75	£58.74

Task 3

	VAT	Insurance	Total
Slapshot	£7.52	1.01	£51.52
Super 9	£8.75	1.17	£59.91
Trident	£7.00	0.94	£47.93
Terminator	£8.75	1.17	£59.91

Unit 30 Information technology applications

Task 1

Appendix

These are some of the information devices you may have thought could help them complete the stages of their daily tasks:

Job	IT device for capture	IT device for process retrieval	IT device for storage	IT device for communication
Receive Order	Keyboard Fax machine OCR, OMR	Computer system running database application software	Computer with hard disk, magnetic disk, magnetic tape or optical disk	Telephone or fax if required to communicate quickly with customer Printer linked to computer to print lists VDU screen for display
Invoices	Keyboard	Computer system running accounts or spreadsheets application software	Computer with hard disk, magnetic disk, magnetic tape or optical disk	Telephone if required to communicate with customer Printer linked to computer to print out invoices VDU screen for display
Stock records	Keyboard	Computer system running stock control application program	Computer with hard disk, magnetic disk, magnetic tape or optical disk	Printer linked to computer to print out stock lists VDU screen for display
Remittances	Keyboard	Computer system running accounts, spreadsheets or database application software	Computer with hard disk, magnetic disk, magnetic tape or optical disk	Printer linked to computer to print out records of payment VDU screen for display

Index

A
accounting/bookkeeping programs *99*
alignment – text presentation *49*
alphabetic data *46*
applications software packages/programs
 69, 71
 – accounting/bookkeeping *99*
 – choosing *73*
 – command-driven *72*
 – databases *74*
 – desktop publishing *87*
 – development *72*
 – ease of use *72*
 – graphics *87*
 – integrated software *99*
 – menu-driven *72*
 – muscial instrument digital interface *101*
 – spreadsheets *64*
 – word processing *49*

B
backing up data *82*
bar code reader *90*
bits *57*
bold – text enhancement *50*
bookkeeping/accounting programs *99*
bubblejet printer *93*
bytes *56, 57*

C
CD-ROM *78*
cells – spreadsheets *64*
cellular telephones *94*
central processing unit *57, 59*
centred – text presentation *49*
charts and graphs – spreadsheets *67*
chip
 – microprocessor *57*
 – Intel *59*
 – Motorola *61*
ClipArt *87*
command-driven *70, 72*
communication technology *94*
 – cellular telephones *94*
 – electronic mail *94*
 – facsimile (FAX machines) *96*
 – public telephone network *95*
 – tele/video conferencing *97*
 – telex *97*
 – videotext *97*
 – on-line databases *97*
computer development *58*
copying text *50*

cutting text *50*

D
Data Protection Act *77*
Data Protection Principles *77*
Data Register *77*
data *46*
data capture *46*
 devices *46*
data communication devices *49*
data processing *46*
 devices *48*
data security *80*
 – administrative controls *82*
 – backing up *82*
 – hackers *80*
 – passwords *80*
 – software controls *80*
 – viruses *82*
 –physical controls *80*
data storage devices *49*
data storage media *78*
 – hard disks *78*
 – optical disks *78*
databases *74*
 – benefits *75*
 – Data Protection Act *77*
 – definition *74*
 – fields *74*
 – key fields *74*
 – on-line *97*
 – records *74*
 – reports *76*
 – searches *75*
 – sorts *75*
dedicated word processor *52*
desktop publishing (DTP) *87*
 – frame-based packages *88*
 – paste-board packages *89*
 – types of program *88*
digitising graphics tablet *91*
disks
 – floppy *54*
 – formatting *55*
 – hard *76*
 – initialisation *55*
display monitors *61*
dot matrix printers *93*
draw packages *84*
DTP (desktop publishing) *87*

E
electronic mail *94*

Index

F
facsimile (FAX) machines *96*
fields – databases *74*
file address track (FAT) *55*
floppy disks *54*
formatting disks *55*
formatting text *50*
formula – spreadsheets *65*
frame-bases packages *88*
G
graphic data *46*
graphical user interface (GUI) *70*
graphics packages/programs *84*
   – ClipArt *87*
graphs and charts – spreadsheets *67*
H
hackers *80*
hard disk *78*
   – read/write heads *78*
hardware *56*
   development *58*
   – mainframe *58*
   – micro-computer *59*
   – mini-computer *58*
health and safety *83*
   – repetitive strain injury *83*
I
icons *70*
information *46*
   – communicating *46*
   – storing and retrieving *46*
   – technology and *48*
information processing *46*
   – the four stages *47*
information technology – further applications (domestic, military, educational, etc) *102*
inkjet printers *93*
input devices *90*
integrated software packages/programs *99*
   – choosing *100*
Intel chips *59*
italic – text enhancement *50*
J
justified – text presentation *49*
K
key fields – databases *74*
kilobyte (kb) *56, 57*
Kimball tag reader *91*
L
laser printers *93*

layout – text *50*
legislation
   – Data Protection Act *77*
   – Data Protection Principles *77*
   – Data Register *77*
light pen *91*
M
macros *51, 54, 67, 73*
magnetic ink character reader *91*
magnetic tape *79*
magneto-optical disks *79*
mailmerge *51*
mainframe computer *58*
margins *51*
megabyte (mb) *56, 57*
Megahertz (Mhz) *59*
memory
   – bits *57*
   – bytes, kilobytes, megabytes *56, 57*
   – microprocessor *57*
   – random access memory (RAM) *57*
   – read only memory (ROM) *57*
menu *58*
menu-driven *72*
Mhz (Megahertz) *59*
micro-computer *59*
microprocessor *57*
   – central processing unit *57, 59*
   chip *57*
   families *59*
   – Intel chips *59*
   – Megahertz *59*
   – Motorola chips *61*
   – memory *57*
mini-computer *58*
modelling – spreadsheets *66*
monitors *61*
   – resolution *62*
   – pixels *62*
Motorola chips *61*
mouse *70, 91*
MSDOS *70*
muscial instrument digital interface (MIDI) *101*

O
on-line databases *97*
operating system *69*
   –Apple Macintosh *70*
   – MSDOS *70*
   – UNIX *70*
optical character reader (OCR) *91*

Index

optical disks *78*
   – CD-ROM *78*
optical mark reader (OMR) *91*
output devices – printers *92*

P

paint packages *84*
passwords *80*
paste-board packages *89*
pasting text *50*
PC (personal computer) *59, 70, 71*
pixel *62, 84*
printers *92*
   – bubblejet *93*
   – dot matrix *92*
   – inkjet *93*
   – laser *93*
processors *59*
public telephone network (PTN) *95*

R

random acccess memory (RAM) *57*
read only memory (ROM) *57*
read/write heads *54, 78*
records – databases *74*
reordering text *39*
repetitive strain injury (RSI) *83*
replace text *50*
reports – databases *76*

S

safety and health *83*
scanners *91*
screen *61*
scrolling *64*
search – databases *75*
search text *50*
security – data *66*
software *69*
   – applications programs *69, 71*
   – systems programs *69*
sorts – databases *75*
spell check *51*
spreadsheets *64*
   – choosing *69*
   – cells *64*
   – charts and graphs *67*
   – data types *65*
   – definition *64*
   – formula *65*
   – functions *66*
   – modelling *66*
   – 'what if'analysis *66*
storage – external and internal *57*
system software *69*

   – Apple Macintosh *70*
   – MSDOS *70*
   –UNIX *71*

T

tabulation *50*
tele/video conferencing *97*
telex *97*
text
   – copying *50*
   – cutting *50*
   formatting *50*
   layout *50*
   – margins *51*
   – pasting *50*
   – reordering *50*
   – replace *50*
   – search *50*
   – spell check *51*
   – tabulation *50*
   – thesaurus *51*
text enhancements *50*
   – bold *50*
   – italic *50*
   – typefaces *51*
   – underlining *50*
text presentation *49*
   – alignment *49*
   – centred *49*
   – justified *49*
   – wordwrap *49*
thesaurus – text *51*
typefaces *51*

U

underlining – text enhancement *50*
UNIX *71*

V

videotext *97*
viruses *82*
VDU (visual display unit) *61, 83*

W

'what if' analysis – spreadsheets *66*
Winchester (hard) disk *78*
Windows *59, 71, 100*
word processing *49*
word processor
   – choosing *52*
   – dedicated *52*
   – different types *52*
wordwrap – text presentation *49*
WYSIWYG (What You See Is What You Get) *52*

Discovering the World of Business
An Active-Learning Approach

J Hillas

ISBN: 1 85805 005 7 • Date: July 1993 • Edition: 1st
Extent: 350 pp (approx) • Size: 275 x 215 mm

> *Courses on which this book is expected to be used*
>
> Intermediate GNVQ in business BTEC First Business and Finance (core), GCSE Business Studies, RSA, CPVE or for students following Business Administration NVQ 2

This book provides all the teaching material needed for students following the new Intermediate GNVQ in Business and equivalent courses. It is divided into three main sections, which enable the student first to identify the 'problem' in a realistic business setting (Section 1 – Scenarios and Related Tasks), then to acquire the necessary skills and principles to solve it (Section 2 – Information Bank) and finally to extend their understanding through further activities and assignments (Section 3 – Developing Knowledge and Skills).

Contents:

Section 1 – Peachtree Computers Ltd
26 units centred around Peachtree Computers Ltd, in which the student deals with all the work tasks expected of an office admin trainee.

Section 2 – Information Bank

The Business World: World Economies. Location of Industry. The Environment. The Government and its Effect on Organisations. The European Community. The Court System.

Business Organisations: Business Organisations. Business Goals and Objectives. Organisational Structure. Researching and Presenting Information.

Business Communications: Introduction to Communication. Business Letters. Memorandums. Reports. Presentations. Business Meetings. Telephone Communications. Noticeboards, Questionnaires and Forms.

People in Business: Why People Work. Typical Job Roles and Functions. Organisation Culture. Introduction to Human Resource Management. Recruitment and Selection. Induction and Training. The Employment Contract. Equal Opportunities. Personnel Records. Payment Systems and Administration. Introduction to Trade Unions. The Importance of Team Work. Health and Safety in the Workplace.

Financial and Business Resources: Making the Most of Business Resources. Sources of Finance for Business. The Banking System. Business Costs. How Money Works in Business. An Introduction to Financial Documentation. Petty Cash. Stock Records. The Financial Recording System. Simple Final Accounts. Value Added Tax.

Customers: Consumer Protection Laws. Customer Care. Marketing.

People, Technology and Change: Office Technology. The Computer. An Introduction to Business Software Packages. Organisations and Change.

Administrative Systems: Filing Systems and Methods. Mail Handling. Reprographics.

Section 3 – Projects for Further Practice & Development
Projects include: Company Policy Handbook; Organisational Structure; The Business Organisation; A Suitable Location; World Economies; A Day on Reception; An Environmental Audit; Into Europe; Business Communications; Protecting the Consumer; Equal Opportunities; Health and Safety Awareness; Trade Union Issues; Office Equipment; Back in the Mail Room; Marketing; Petty Cash; Keeping Financial Records; Back in the Stores; Wages; Careers Portfolio; An Exhibition; Using a Spreadsheet Package; In the Personnel Department; Setting up a Small Business; Accounts; Privatisation; Training.

Appendix • Answers to tasks in Section 1.

♠ **Free Lecturers' Supplement** ♠

Advanced Level Business Studies
An Active-Learning Approach

S Danks

ISBN: 1 85805 016 2 • Date: July 1993 • Edition: 1st
Extent: 400 pp (approx) • Size: 275 x 215 mm

Courses on which this book is expected to be used
Advanced GNVQ, A Level Business Studies and other business studies courses at this level

---

The aim of this book is to provide complete coverage of the new Business Advanced GNVQ and A Level Business Studies, and will be appropriate for many business courses at this level. It allows lecturers to recommend a **single textbook** to cover the **whole of the core syllabus** for A Level as well as the mandatory units of Business GNVQs (as indicated in a syllabus analysis grid), and gives students **concise information** on the themes, knowledge and skills required. All chapters include **self-assessment tasks, summaries, review questions, examination practice questions** and **assignment activities.**

It covers the major business themes including organisations and goals, marketing, financial resources, human resources, physical resources, administrative systems and innovation and change.

Case studies and research projects feature prominently throughout the text.

Contents:

The Business Environment • Business Enterprise • External Influences on Business • The Market Mechanism • Business and the Economy
• Marketing and Market Research • The Marketing Mix – Product and Price • The Marketing Mix – Promotion and Place • Business Finance
• Financial Record Keeping • Business Performance • Human Resources in Organisations • Organisational Behaviour; Employer and Employee Relations • Production Processes and Control • Business and International Economy • Business Information Systems • Innovation and Change • Data Analysis and Presentation • Starting and Running Your Own Business

---

♠ **Free Lecturers' Supplement** ♠

A First Course in Statistics

DJ Booth

ISBN: 1 873981 14 7 • Date: 1992 • Edition: 2nd
Extent: 304 pp • Size: 245 x 190 mm

> *Courses on which this book is known to be used*
> BTEC Business and Secretarial Studies; RSA; LCCI; AAT Certificate; ACCA; CIMA; IPS; IPM; DMS; BA Public Administration; Institute of Export.
>
> **On reading lists of LCCI and ICM**

This book provides a core text for introductory level courses in statistics. It assumes the student has no prior knowledge of statistics whatsoever and no more than an ability to handle simple arithmetic.

The second edition includes a section on elementary inferential statistics and has extended end of unit exercises.

Contents:

This is Statistics • Fundamental Ideas • Asking the Question • Collecting the Data • Deriving the Statistics • Communicating the Results • **Asking Questions** • Questions and Statistics • Who Asks the Questions • How to Ask Questions • How Not to Ask Questions • Questionnaire Design • When to Ask Questions • **Collection of Data** • Primary Data • Probability and Sampling • Organising the Data • Tabulation of Data • Secondary Data • Graphical Representation of Data • **Deriving the Statistics** • Single Statistics • Dispersion • Multiple Statistics • Index Numbers • Regression • Correlation • Time Series • **Communicating the Results** • The General Principles of Presentation • Demonstration Tables • Pictorial Representation • The Use of Words • **Inferential Statistics** • Sets and Random Experiments • Probabilities and Combinatorics • Probability Distributions • Sampling Distributions • Hypothesis Testing • Statistical Tables • Answers to Exercises.

Review Comments:

'The book is a breath of fresh air to those who think statistics is an essentially practical subject.'
　　　　　　　　　　　　　　　　　　　　　　　　　　　　　　　　　　　　　"The Mathematical Gazette"

'Well set out, with clear and concise and relevant explanations – best book I have seen.' 'It is simple, systematic, logical and not pretentious.' 'Only book I have come across which does not become too complicated for non-numerate social science students.'
　　　– *Lecturers*

♠ **Free Lecturers' Supplement** ♠

A First Course in
Cost and Management Accounting

T Lucey

ISBN: 1 85805 014 6 • Date: June 1993 • Edition: 2nd
Extent: 272 pp (approx) • Size: 245 x 190 mm

> *Courses on which this book is known to be used*
>
> BTEC National Business and Finance; DMS; RSA; LCCI; AAT; CIPFA; Management and Supervisory Studies; Business Studies and Marketing courses; Access courses; Purchasing and Supply and other courses requiring a broad, non-specialist treatment of cost and management accounting.

This book provides a broad introduction to cost and management accounting for those who have not studied the subject before. It is written in a clear, straightforward fashion without technical jargon or unnecessary detail.

The Second Edition includes numerous extensions of coverage including ABC, JIT and other developments, costing in service and not-for-profit organisations, behavioural aspects of budgeting etc.

The text includes practical examples, diagrams, exercises, objective tests and examination questions.

Contents:

Cost Analysis and Cost Ascertainment • What is Product Costing and Cost Accounting? • Elements of Cost • Labour, Materials and Overheads • Calculating Product Costs • Job, Batch and Contract Costing • Service, Process and Joint Product Costing • Information for Planning and Control • What is Planning and Control? • Cost Behaviour • Budgetary Planning • Budgetary Control • Cash Budgeting • Standard Costing • Variance Analysis • Information for Decision Making and Performance Appraisal • What is Decision Making? • Marginal Costing • Break-even Analysis • Pricing Decisions • Investment Appraisal • Performance Appraisal of Departments and Divisions.

Review Comments:

"Excellent beginners text.' – Lecturer

♠ Free Lecturers' Supplement ♠